SMART
WORK

STEVEN A. STANTON

Smart Work: Why Organizations Full of Intelligent People Do So Many Dumb Things and What You Can Do About It

For information visit:
Smartwork.work

Cover design by Asha Hossein

Book design by Sue Balcer / JustYourType.biz

Library of Congress Cataloging-in-Publication Data

Steven A. Stanton

ISBN 978-0-9980822-0-2

PRINTED IN THE UNITED STATES OF AMERICA

First Edition: October 2016

10 9 8 7 6 5 4 3 2 1

Text for this book was set in Acumin Pro.

SMART WORK

WHY ORGANIZATIONS FULL OF INTELLIGENT PEOPLE DO SO MANY DUMB THINGS, AND WHAT *YOU* CAN DO ABOUT IT

STEVEN A. STANTON

CO-AUTHOR OF *THE REENGINEERING REVOLUTION*

To Pat, Alec, and Graham

Preface
Observations of an Industrial Tourist

Thank you for opening this book. I appreciate your joining me here.

I've had the pleasure over the past 30 years of being a visitor to hundreds of organizations. As a consultant, teacher, public speaker, and researcher, my work on improving performance has allowed me to learn how many organizations work, and how they don't.

As a perpetual guest, I've seen how smart employees get frustrated by the invisible barriers that limit their initiative and offer little space for ingenuity. This same problem exists in countless organizations of every scale, in every sector. No one is immune to organizational resistance to change.

Those, like you, who sincerely want to improve their organizations face formidable barriers, and this book is intended to help you overcome them. It's tough being an advocate for change in an organization that's stuck in the status quo. I hope this book helps or at least lets you know you're not alone.

You're busy, so I've tried to keep this book short and easy to read. Having read, or tried to read, many business books, I know that many are little more than puffed-up articles, over-stuffed with long case studies. Of course I've used real-life stories, but I've kept them short. In most cases, the names have been disguised to protect the guilty. My long subtitle may seem awkward, but as with many new concepts, there's no tidy word or phrase that expresses my basic idea.

Twenty-five years ago, one of my mentors, Dr. Michael Hammer, said something that never left me, *"It's when you're the most comfortable, or the least worried, that you're the most vulnerable. The unexamined company doesn't stand a chance."* By paraphrasing Plato, he was talking about the need for organizations to get smarter and to liberate their employees to use the bounty of data that's now available to do better work for customers.

This book begins with an all-out assault on the many dumb things organizations do. In my experience, many organizations behave in ways that, if they were individuals, would get them fired.

It has never been the case that employees within an enterprise are stupid. They're not. You're not. Dysfunctions within the traditional organizational model have dumbed them down.

It's time for you to unleash that intelligence and Get Smart.

Enjoy the book.

Steve Stanton
September 2016
Boston, Massachusetts

OVERVIEW

"We cannot solve our problems with the same thinking we used when we created them."

ALBERT EINSTEIN

Why do organizations full of intelligent people do so many dumb things?

That's the question this book will attempt to answer. The short response is that large traditional organizations are prisoners of the past. They're frozen in an old organizational model that no longer fits today's competitive marketplaces. Worse, they're not truly aware of how stuck they've become. They keep trying the same old conventional ways to change, to no avail. Mergers and acquisitions are on the rise, as is the rate of organizational restructuring, but neither addresses the root problem. The problem is not at the surface but at the core.

The old model contains many invisible barriers to effective change. Causes of inefficiency such as email overload and bad meetings eat up precious work hours. Responsibility for them doesn't fit within the conventional paradigm. Festering dysfunctions, parts of the hidden logic of the business, are perpetuated because *"That's the way we've always done it."* For these organizations, action replaces reflection and the urgent drives out the important.

Worse, the old model cannot accommodate the talents of employees and dumbs them down. Old-fashioned role definitions restrict employees' ability to contribute. *"I check my brain at the gate,"* is the sad refrain of unengaged workers.

Traditional organizations have developed formidable defenses against the very changes they need for survival. Strong internal boundaries inhibit collaboration and drive up costs and wasted time. Unclear roles and decision rights diffuse the power of integration. For all their assets, large organizations are weaker than the sum of their parts because the basic design of the industrial-era organization was explicitly intended to limit change and innovation. Hierarchy and strong silos are inherent constraints.

Every one of these problems drives the organization's energy internally. The result is less time, energy, attention, and resources for customers. It's a doom loop.

Only by accepting the transformational change driven by a new data-driven nervous system can traditional organizations use their assets to win. That requires rethinking measurement, external sensing, and how they go about improvement. When they exploit data better, they can achieve a new level of consciousness and achieve higher levels of performance.

When they don't, they're doomed to decline. *Smart Work* is designed to help organizations avoid that fate.

Contents

Preface: Observations of an Industrial Tourist..vi

Overview..ix

PART 1: WHAT GETS IN THE WAY?

1. TOO BUSY TO THINK 3

- ENDLESS EMAIL... 3
- MEETING MADNESS... 6
- PROJECT-ITIS 8
- WHY IS EVERYONE SO BUSY?..9
- WHEN YOU'RE 2BZ2 THINK.. 10
- IT'S A TERRIBLE TIME TO BE DUMB................................. 11
- PUNCTUATED EQUILIBRIUM 13

2. SEVEN DEADLY DYSFUNCTIONS 15

- 1. URGENCY.. 17
- 2. MORE!.. 19
- 3. SUPERFICIALITY 21
- 4. OBLIVIOUSNESS...23
- 5. NARCISSISM: LET'S TALK ABOUT ME............................25
- 6. NOW: IMMEDIATE GRATIFICATION 28
- 7. LOCALISM...32

PART 2: THE SHAPE OF THE SOLUTION

3. BECOMING A SMART ORGANIZATION: FROM VICTIM TO VICTOR 39

- DATA, DATA, EVERYWHERE 39
- YOU CAN'T GET THERE FROM HERE 40
- FLYING FROM LINE OF SIGHT TO INSTRUMENTATION ...42
- DATA ALCHEMY 44
- FROM AVERAGES TO ACTUALS 45
- HANSEI OR THE ART OF REFLECTION..............................46

PART 3: GETTING SMARTER

4. SMART METRICS: FROM GUESSING TO KNOWING 51

- MEASUREMENT EXCELLENCE IS TOUGH......52
- FIVE WAYS TO FAIL AT MEASUREMENT......53
- SMART MEASUREMENT......55
- UNDERSTANDING THE TRUE PURPOSES OF MEASUREMENT......57
- IDENTIFYING THE RIGHT METRICS......58
- SETTING PERFORMANCE TARGETS......63
- DEVELOPING AN EFFECTIVE MEASUREMENT CYCLE......64
- EVOLVING MEASUREMENT......66

5. SMART SENSING: FROM INSIDE TO OUTSIDE 69

- FAST FASHION......70
- FOCUSING OUTSIDE......72
- CUSTOMER QUESTIONS......74
- COMPETITOR QUESTIONS......75
- LOOKING THROUGH THE JOHARI WINDOW......76
- SENSING STORY......78
- THE LOST CUSTOMER AUDIT......80
- THROW YOUR EXECUTIVES OUT INTO THE MARKETPLACE....80
- IN THE CROW'S NEST: DISRUPTOR PARANOIA......82
- TRADITIONAL COMPETITOR SENSING: EXTREME VERSION......82
- MARKET SENSING TACTICS FOR CUSTOMER INSIGHT......83
- MARKET SENSING TACTICS FOR COMPETITOR INSIGHTS......84
- ENVIRONMENTAL SENSING......84
- THE PROCESS OF SENSING......84
- THE ZEN OF SENSING......85

6. THE IMPERATIVES OF SMART IMPROVEMENT: FROM BETTER SAMENESS TO TRANSFORMATION......87

- KNOCK DOWN YOUR SILOS......87
- EMBRACE TRANSFORMATIONAL CHANGE......92
- DO FEWER BUT BETTER PROJECTS......101
- DIGITIZE YOUR PROCESSES......105
- MAKE DATA-DRIVEN DECISIONS......108

7. SMARTER WORKERS: FROM TAYLOR TO TOMORROW 111

- 1. INSPIRE THEM WITH A POWERFUL PURPOSE 114
- 2. TURN THEM INTO PROFESSIONALS BY MAKING THEIR JOBS BIGGER 117
- 3. INVOLVE EVERYONE IN CHANGE 121
- 4. EDUCATE THEM ABOUT THE BUSINESS..122
- 5. LIBERATE EVERYONE FROM OUTMODED POLICIES 125
- FREEDOM AND TIME TO THINK...128
- SMART MEETINGS 128
- SMART EMAIL..132

8. SMART BEHAVIORS: FROM WORDS TO ACTIONS 135

- 1. COMPLETELY CUSTOMER-CENTRIC..136
- 2. AMBITIOUS YET HUMBLE 137
- 3. DOUBLY ACCOUNTABLE 138
- 4. DECISIVE AND DATA DRIVEN...140
- 5. COLLABORATIVE TOGETHER...142
- 6. INTELLECTUALLY CURIOUS 143
- FINAL EXAM..146

9. SMART ENTERPRISE: FROM FEUDALISM TO FEDERALISM..147

- THE FUTILITY OF FEUDALISM 149
- FEDERALISM IS NEEDED 150
- FROM CONGLOMERATE TO FEDERALIST 152
- GOVERNING PROCESSES 153
- STRATEGIC PLANNING AND THE THREE GREAT TENSIONS....154
- WHO DO YOU SERVE? 156
- STRATEGIC PRINCIPLES 157
- TODAY VS. TOMORROW 159
- STRATEGIC EXECUTION...161

10. SMART YOU 165

Acknowledgments...169

PART 1: WHAT GETS IN THE WAY?

CHAPTER ONE
TOO BUSY TO THINK

Are you busy?

In a typical encounter, when you ask someone how they're doing, the answer is likely to be "Busy."

Busyness is the prevailing condition of our times. We have long to-do lists that never get completed. The pace of work is relentless, and as soon as one task is done, two more are thrown over the transom and have to be done by the end of the day. There's so much to do and so little time to do it. A December 2015 Gallup poll found that 61 percent of American workers said they didn't ever have enough time to do the things they needed to do.

A perfect metaphor for the busyness of work life is the carnival game "Whack-a-Mole," where, armed with a rubber mallet, you attempt to batter down plastic moles as they emerge, faster and faster, from holes in the machine. Although it may be emotionally satisfying to hammer down those little buggers, you can never ever win. They just keep coming with an unpredictable ferocity. Just like your workload.

But where does all this busyness come from? Let's see if the following three time-sucking culprits can explain your situation.

ENDLESS EMAIL

On an average work day, how many email messages do you receive? 50? 100? 300? Too busy plowing through them to count?

Whatever the number, it's bound to be big.

In 2012, *Fortune* Magazine reported that American workers

were spending 28 percent of their time plowing through email. The *Harvard Business Review* stated in 2013 that, on average, 111 business days per year were spent on email communications.

Whew!

According to the Radicati Group, by 2015, 2.6 billion emails were sent per day worldwide with that number expected to rise by 3 percent per year. DMR research states that in 2015 the average worker received more than 121 emails per day, often requiring 3 to 4 hours to slog through their daily haul.

These numbers just reflect email. In addition, American workers now have to contend with instant messaging, social media, and plain old telephone calls.

Communications is exploding everywhere, not just at your desk. In 2015, the Max Planck Institute for Informatics found that the average number of smartphone checks per person was 46 per day, with millennials clocking in at 74 times a day.

This reflexive communication checking is so pervasive that there's a new medical phenomenon, "vibrating thigh," the feeling that your phone is pulsing, despite the fact that it's in your shirt, purse, or attaché.

For most workers, regardless of rank, communication fills every crack and crevice of their calendar, seeping into every spare moment. By keeping our phones on and responding when they demand attention, we're giving tacit permission to senders that it's OK to send messages at any hour of the day. Response is expected. For 62 percent of us, checking email is the last thing we do before sleep and the first thing we do upon waking.

What's causing this email tsunami? For starters, email is an unprecedented technology. The world has never experienced a free, always on, many-to-many communication media before. Previous communication technologies such as snail mail and telephone were one-to-one and incurred a cost to the sender. These limitations constrained traditional communication. But no longer, because there's no marginal cost difference between sending to one recipient or to 100. As a result, there are billions of email messages flying around the world every week, and an explosion of emails from vast distribution lists clogs our in-boxes.

Email has made us all screen zombies. Next time you're walking down the street or in an elevator, check out where people's attention is focused. We've become prisoners of our own devices.

Email is draining away work hours from every employee in every organization. When you're heads down on email, you can't be heads up solving problems. Add up all the hours spent on email, and the productivity loss is staggering. Instead of delighting customers or improving processes, employees are glued to their screens busily deleting irrelevant email. What a waste.

Worse, the email mess is a huge problem **nobody owns**. It's both invisible to the organization and overwhelming to employees. Who's responsible for email in your organization? Whose problem is this? Who's measured or incentivized to solve email madness? Probably no one. Or everyone. Or your CEO or CIO, who just may have a few other more strategic, pressing issues on their plate.

Email is an organizational orphan. It doesn't fit neatly anywhere in traditional models. It's pervasive and causes a humongous productivity problem, yet it's homeless.

To keep on doing nothing about a problem of this scale is just plain dumb.

MEETING MADNESS

On top of all that communication, how many hours each week do you spend attending meetings? If you're like most employees the answer is *"Too many!"* You have team meetings, project meetings, status meetings, update meetings, standup meetings, and meetings to plan meetings. The variety is endless, as are many of the meetings themselves.

The Atlassian Group estimates that the average American worker attends 62 meetings per month, which computes to more than 3 meetings a day—a major portion of everyone's workday.

How many of your meetings are productive encounters that deeply engage you and produce meaningful results?

Atlassian's research reveals that 50 percent of all meetings are considered ineffective "wasted time" meetings (which personally I believe is far too low an estimate). Another perspective comes from Jim Ware, whose recent book is *Making Meetings Matter.* He estimates that 90 percent of all meetings are dysfunctional. At one hour per meeting, that wasted time equals 18 percent of the average workweek of every employee.

Which means that it's both the quantity and the quality of meetings that's problematic.

There are so many ways to have a bad meeting. Many meetings have no clear purpose or meaningful agenda. Frequently, agenda items offer no clarity on the topic's purpose, so attendees have no clue if the issue that's on the table is for update or decision. When meeting discipline is mostly absent, these problems occur:

- The entire meeting is spent on the first agenda topic

- The meeting starts and ends later than advertised

- Action items are hopeful wishes

Any of this familiar to you? Of course it's not just you.

This problem is even worse for executives, who, according to Atlassian, often spend 40 to 50 percent of their time in meetings; for them, the costs of bad meetings is far higher.

David Grady in his TED talk, estimated that bad meetings cost US companies a staggering $37 billion a year. For every Fortune 50 company, that works out to $75 million a year down the drain.

The authors also state that 73 percent of meeting attendees spend long stretches daydreaming during their meetings. Many others are preoccupied by their smartphones, whittling down their email stack. This is so pervasive that one of the most common comments one hears in meetings is, *"Can you please repeat that?"* spoken when an attendee hears their name but hasn't been paying attention.

If asked, these attendees claim that they're *"multitasking,"* which is just another way of describing how to fail at several things simultaneously.

Worse yet, the TED talk cited earlier mentions the sobering fact that 75 percent of American organizations did not offer training on effective meeting management, despite the fact that the rules for running a good meeting are relatively well known and not all that difficult to execute.

Nevertheless, organizations continue to generate and require that employees attend more and more meetings. It's crazy. As the author Rita Mae Brown once said, *"Insanity is doing the same thing over and over again and expecting a different result each time."* But perhaps it's not so strange after all.

Who's responsible for meeting management in your organization? Perhaps the same person that owns email. It's another orphan, dispersed, destructive, and homeless. And another productivity drain.

Why do organizations continue to hold so many terrible

meetings? Why do smart people allow this obvious problem to persist?

It's just dumb.

PROJECT-ITIS

There's a new malady contributing to business busyness, Project-itis. This occurs when organizations launch an endless stream of disconnected change projects. Because there's no central repository of project data, there's absolutely no way for these projects to be counted, prioritized, rationalized, or aligned. It's not surprising then that many of these dispersed projects are redundant or in direct conflict. There's just no way to tell.

When Project-itis occurs, no one knows the total investment the organization is making under the banner of improvement. It's an **invisible** but huge sum. Even worse, because there's no clear project inventory, the organization has no way to align its project managers to the right task, track overall success rates, or conduct consistent post-project reviews.

While these projects are hopefully motivated by a sincere intent to improve performance, the execution is pure chaos. Project-itis stems from unbound freedom, where anyone can launch a project at any time. And because they can, they do. The result is a blizzard of change efforts. As George Bernard Shaw once noted, *"The road to hell is paved with good intentions."*

Because the costs of these projects are invisible to everyone, organizations spend with wild abandon. They behave as if they have unlimited resources to spend and an infinite ability to absorb change. Neither is true.

Of course Project-itis contributes to busyness in other ways as well, as all these project teams hold frequent meetings and email each other endlessly.

Taken together, Email Mania, Meeting Madness, and Project-itis consume huge portions of every employee's productive time. As one manager sadly explained, *"4 p.m. is when I start doing real work."*

Why do organizations allow these productivity disasters to persist?

WHY IS EVERYONE SO BUSY?

What's behind all of this busyness?   What's driving all this communication? Why now?

The first cause of widespread busyness is the relentless **downsizing** of the past 20 years. Repeated cost management purges have left many organizations anorexic. In a 2012 Fortune magazine article, a Walmart senior executive sadly admitted, *"We have cut costs too far, stores are understaffed, and associates cannot provide customers the service that Sam Walton built the company on."*

Sometimes called layoffs, RIFs, headcount adjustments, or drive-by-shootings, these employee-reduction programs have often been focused on the bottom of the organization, where frontline workers have the least power and most vulnerability.

There's ample data to prove that layoffs simply don't work. They don't provide substantial and lasting cost reduction. Sadly, most of these efforts simply reduce the total number of workers, but never adjust the quality or quantity of the work that needs to be performed. For example, at one very large chemical company, the same amount of work that was done five years ago is now done with one-third fewer employees. The tasks never disappeared, only the workers did, and the survivors are busier than ever—augmented by rehired ex-employees who now serve as expensive consultants.

The last 20 years' devotion to the principles of shareholder value and its evil twin, short-term-quarterly-returns-to-make-Wall-Street-happy, have driven cost-reduction pogroms to extremes, thinning out the workforce and increasing every survivor's busyness.

The second driver of busyness is the intensified level of competition in every sector, facing every organization. No one is immune. Technology and globalization have raised the competitive stakes for everyone. Local markets have disappeared and everyone is competing against their best global competitors.

The third contributor to busyness is the explosion of new technologies: artificial intelligence, inexpensive sensors and the Internet of Things (IoT), SaaS in the cloud, mobile, social, etc. We're surrounded by massive amounts of data, and all of these new tools offer opportunities to produce, receive, and analyze data. All of which take time. Lots of time.

It's a simple formula. As the amount of work increases, and the number of workers decreases, and there are new tools to learn, everyone gets busier and busier. The McKinsey Quarterly found that 60 percent of the average workday was spent on email and meetings alone. It's a trap. The busier you are, the less time you have to figure out how to escape that busyness.

WHEN YOU'RE 2BZ2 THINK

So what does all of this busyness leave you no time for? I've been asking my clients and students this question for many years, and their answers tend to be consistent:

- No time for my job
- No time for my customers
- No time for managing my boss
- No time for work-life balance

These are reasonable and truthful answers, but they leave the most important loss unsaid: The biggest casualty is that it leaves us with **no time to think!**

When you're crossing things off your endless to-do list, fighting fires, and dealing with surprise work thrown at you at the last minute, there's never a quiet moment to sit back and think. There's no time to reflect on what you just accomplished, because the next three pieces of work have just arrived and they're all due yesterday.

When you're too busy to think, action is king. Motion is valued over reflection, and endless execution enhances your career. It's an "on-to-the-next thing" merry-go-round, perpetually spinning, with no way to get off.

A 2013 survey by the Energy Project of 12,115 workers worldwide found that 70 percent had no regular time for creative thinking and 66 percent didn't have the ability to focus on one thing at a time.

And reflection can be dangerous if sitting quietly at your desk, deep in thought, makes your manager worry that you don't have enough to do.

When you're too busy to think, intelligence suffers, insights are lost, and you act dumber than you really are.

When you're frantic, there's less time to creatively generate customer delight or to discover the next breakthrough product or process. Instead of spending time on creating value, you're trapped whacking down those pesky moles.

IT'S A TERRIBLE TIME TO BE DUMB

In every sector of our economy, organizations are experiencing a trifecta of speed, complexity, and novelty. This external turbulence is unprecedented.

No matter what its cause, the metabolism of business is

quickening as transactions, communications, and decisions happen more rapidly than ever. It took 22 years after its introduction to the market for fax technology to reach a million users, and it took six years for personal computers to reach the same milestone. These days, it seems like it can take 15 minutes for a new app to reach the same number of users.

Everything is accelerated, but when you're making fast decisions, are you making smart ones?

In the same way, complexity is growing exponentially. With more choices everywhere, from suppliers to partners to technologies, the global economy is ever more connected and complicated. This intricacy of most markets is growing faster than our ability to understand it.

When do you take the time to unravel all your complexity?

On top of this is the fact that most organizations are facing challenges they've never seen before. Email, global supply chains, outsourcing, and insourcing are all relatively unprecedented issues. Instead of problems you've faced before, you're increasingly confronted by new ones that offer no easy answers.

Without history to guide you, are you taking enough time to think these new challenges through?

The risks of today's environmental turbulence are particularly acute for traditional, industrial era organizations. When grand old organizations succumb to busyness, the symptoms are exponentially worse.

Traditional organizations have deep hierarchies, entrenched management paradigms, strong functional silos, and long memories—all of which serve as constraints against change. It's tough to be nimble when you have a 10-layer hierarchy. It's nearly impossible to repudiate your past when you have a history of success.

Look at the accelerating rate of turnover in the Fortune 500.

Busyness causes organizations full of intelligent people to do stupid things, over and over. **When organizations emphasize execution over reflection**, they're on the fast track to failure.

Industrial-era organizations are at risk of being outcompeted by faster, smarter disruptors, just as Neanderthals were outcompeted by Homo Sapiens. If organizations continue to be dumber than their employees, they too will eventually become extinct.

PUNCTUATED EQUILIBRIUM

Most people tend to think that the number of animal species alive at any one time is growing ever larger. That's not true. Speciation, as this number is called, has seen many large swings where, at a single point in time, a large number of living species disappear quickly. This often occurs when environmental change is the greatest.

Just like now.

An organization that cannot solve its self-inflicted productivity problems is stuck because busyness saps the energy needed for escape. **An organization that merely executes is doomed to failure**. It's really dumb to continue to operate in an environment where there's no time to think. Busyness can be fatal.

CHAPTER TWO
SEVEN DEADLY DYSFUNCTIONS

The order is rapidly fading,
And the first one now will later be last.
For the times they are a-changing.

—BOB DYLAN

When the Old Organization meets the New Environment, traditional behaviors prevail. It's a brutal mismatch: a clash of eras and a misalignment of models. In the end, the old way must adapt or wither away. There's no alternative.

When traditional industrial-era organizations, whose basic design was created more than 100 years ago, try to operate in today's disruptive environment, the very characteristics that once produced growth and strength are now the source of weaknesses that challenge their survival.

As a result, traditional organizations with long histories and deep hierarchies are having a tough time adjusting and succeeding in today's world. Command-and-control solutions no longer fit an agile world.

Objects at rest tend to stay at rest. Organizations that haven't embraced constant change tend to resist change. This inertia has flash frozen them with archaic elements such as:

- Old models of manager and worker roles that limit the expansion of knowledge-work jobs

- Outmoded paradigms of information technology that constrain the rapid exploitation of new technologies

- Counterproductive memories of failure that produce stultifying risk-aversion behaviors

- Multiple layers of stodgy hierarchy that slow progress to a standstill

- Incentive designs that are so top-heavy that they alienate employees and further lower engagement

With business models designed for stability, organizations are now struggling to create new futures for themselves in today's turbulent environment. As a senior manager in a large financial services organization lamented, *"We're just a giant status quo machine."*

Think about your organization. How many yes's are needed to approve a change and how many no's can kill one? If yours is like many traditional organizations, the answers are *"many"* and *"one."* Your organization was built to suppress change, not embrace it.

From an archaeological perspective, the organizational model that traditional organizations inherited is predicated on early 20th-century ideas and capabilities. When Taylor, Ford, and Sloan were inventing the "modern" corporation, the dominant paradigm was The Machine. This pervasive metaphor shaped the underlying design of the modern enterprise. With this manufacturing mentality, the modern organization was conceived as a well-designed engine that would smoothly operate in stable, slow-changing environments.

A motto for the old model could well be TTWWADI, or *"That's the Way We've Always Done It."* That's the sound of yesterday overwhelming tomorrow.

The Machine Model served many businesses well for decades, through wars and economic cycles. Then it ran out of gas. The conflict between operating model and environment has become dangerous.

Yesterday's bad habits have become today's dysfunctions. They're systemic but not personal. These patterns of behavior are invisible but pervasive, and they shape the behaviors of uncounted workers unconsciously. The shared industrial model of how things should work has lingered long past its expiration date. The dysfunctions are common to all large organizations that share industrial-era roots. As Stephen Dedalus noted in James Joyce's *Ulysses*, *"History is a nightmare from which I'm trying to awaken."*

These artifacts help explain why organizations full of intelligent people do so many dumb things over and over again. If you look for them in policy manuals, you won't find them. But they're everywhere, shaping behaviors as the unspoken and unwritten rules of the workplace. They're the hidden logic of the organization.

The following seven dysfunctions are divided into two groups, with the first three similar to the notion of venial sins—they'll harm the organization but not destroy it, and the remaining four like mortal sins—if not solved by Smart Work, they will doom the organization to permanent desolation.

1. URGENCY

"Listen, it's urgent that I talk with you right now, it can't possibly wait, it's urgent, so drop whatever it is you're doing and…"

Sound familiar? It's urgent that we talk about all this false urgency.

A terrible consequence of busyness occurs when **the urgent drives out the important.** You can see this problem everywhere: in response to customer demands, when new opportunities suddenly arise, or when someone just needs something done on their timetable. Urgency occurs when the squeaky employee needs your attention right now; when your boss's latest demand trumps your afternoon schedule; when those bastards in accounting have just rejected your expense report for the third time and, unless you follow their inscrutable procedures, you'll never be reimbursed and the deadline is 15 minutes ago.

"Urgency" is now a completely overused and content-free word. When everything is urgent, nothing can be. Many organizations act like Chicken Little, where hundreds of *"urgents"* have neutered the word, and when a real crisis occurs, no one may take it seriously.

Today, it's not enough for you to be busy; urgency demands a frenzy of activity. You can never focus on one task because any moment you'll be interrupted. We live in the age of *Taskus Interruptus*. How many times have you heard something like, *"Urgent, fill that order now or the world as we know it will end."* When you hear the word often enough, urgency becomes meaningless.

How did this ever come to pass? Why do normally sane and intelligent managers behave as if their bowels are in an uproar over every new deadline? How can there actually be an emergency every 30 minutes? What happened to Keep Calm and Carry On? What happened to ready-aim-fire?

Urgency occurs when planning is weak and priorities are murky. When there's no strategic clarity, anything can be called strategic. Or when strategy is a just bunch of clichés, everything is equally important. Behaviorally, no one wants his or her work to be seen as mundane or trivial, so we ratchet up its importance. Urgency validates us, so we push that button again and again. Everyone's a hero or heroine when they solve urgent issues.

Urgency prevails when employees can't or won't differentiate between now or later, the important or the strategic, their priorities or the organization's, their boss's CYA and real work.

Urgency is the bright red warning light that announces *"planning has failed."* It's the triumph of now-ism, when the demands of the current moment are more important than anything else.

On the other hand, in hospitals, there's a reserved word "STAT," which is from the Latin word *statim* (immediately) and implies CRITICAL-RUSH-NOW. It's rarely overused; therefore, it retains meaning. STAT's exclusivity grants it power and compliance. With urgency, it's exactly the opposite.

When the urgent drives out the important, long-term priorities slide down your to-do lists. Your boss's emails become more important than your customers! Tougher tasks never get done.

It's urgent that we get these false emergencies under control.

2. MORE!

Samuel Gompers, the noted American Federation of Labor union leader, was asked during a labor negotiation, what he wanted. He shouted, *"MORE!"*

Gompers would be right at home in most organizations, where nothing ever comes off the table and more work is constantly piled on. Traditional organizations are **additive** and rarely subtractive.

When you're too busy to think or prioritize because everything is urgent, the default is MORE!, which of course makes you even busier and have even less time to think.

It's a thoughtless behavior. It's the opposite of intentional choice. Organizations demand more measures, more projects, more strategic objectives, even more email. It's magical thinking hoping that quantity might transmute into quality. Even our presentations are overstuffed, and there's a new cause of boredom: death by PowerPoint.

When More! prevails, nothing is ever finished, nothing ever disappears, and all efforts are immortal. We end up surrounded by history.

MORE! Is based on the illusion of infinite resources. Apparently, many organizations believe that they can keep piling on work without regard for capacity limitations. Because no one measures or is aware of actual capacities, there's no constraint to constant addition. As a result, MORE! always looks free.

But wait, there's more.

MORE! is suffocating your improvement efforts. As Projectitis adds more improvement projects into the portfolio, you end up with Zombie projects, programs that are dead but don't know it.

For example, at a large chemical company, a major improvement project was launched with team members assigned to the project for 5 percent of their time. That's 2 hours a week. This small percentage was caused by the fact that every member was also participating in several other projects. Ongoing time conflicts caused constant scheduling difficulties; and their next team meeting will be held in February 2028. In the meantime, their project hasn't been declared dead; instead, it just lingers on forever. Between meetings, the members still send updates, but the team produces zero results. Zombie projects don't create value; they just eat resources.

Other manifestation of MORE! include:

- Ghost measures, metrics from the dim past that have never been erased

- Antique reports that are still printed and circulated every Tuesday that haven't been read for years

- Obsolete performance criteria for long-ended jobs

- Unneeded policies and procedures from 50 years ago that molder in unread manuals

All of this debris clogs real work and adds to the busyness doom loop.

You're assumed to have an infinitely expandable personal plate, so when your boss gives you a new assignment, nothing is removed. The understanding is that you'll simply work longer or harder or magically expand your day beyond 24 hours. Based on workloads it appears that today's employees will need three half-time jobs just to keep up.

The Business Roundtable's research indicates that in 2013, the average workweek was 8.5 hours longer than it was in 1979. And the Centers for Disease Control and Prevention estimates that one-third of all working Americans gets less than six hours of sleep a night. More work causes less sleep. MORE! truly is making us work more.

When you suffer from this exhausting form of busyness you're never finished. There are no no's and there's always MORE! to do.

3. SUPERFICIALITY

As a clever executive once declared, *"If you were too busy to get it right the first time, what makes you think you'll ever find time to fix it later?"*

When an organization suffers from superficiality, it manages symptoms instead of solving root problems. When you have no time to dig deep, skimming the surface is the default. Slapping a quick and dirty solution on a problem takes less time when you have none to spare. Cross a to-do off your list, and it's on to the next one. It doesn't matter that the real source of your invoice accuracy problem is an antiquated information system; it's faster and cheaper to develop a work-around instead. You'll get around to the needed system upgrade eventually. Maybe.

When you're too busy to think, you take shortcuts and apply temporary fixes that never go away. You fight fires instead of preventing them. You apply Band-Aids when surgery is needed. You tweak your backhaul planning process instead of redesigning the entire supply chain. You reorganize the purchasing department instead of redesigning the procurement process.

In quality programs, there's a deceptively simple tool called The Five Whys. The idea is to relentlessly ask why until you get to the root cause of the problem. Once you fix the causal problem, the symptoms disappear. But as quality professionals know, when you only treat symptoms, you're just postponing the solution. Consider this Five Whys example from a manufacturing company:

- We missed our production schedule

- Why? The line was down for 2 hours

- Why was the line down? Because the vacuum pump broke

- Why did it break? Because the bearing froze

- Why did it freeze? Because the bearing wasn't greased

- Why not? The preventative maintenance wasn't done

- Why? PM isn't anyone's priority

- Why isn't it? It's not measured or incentivized

It takes time to think through a chain of causation like this. It takes a period of quiet reflection. So when you're overloaded with unending urgent demands, emails, and meetings, it's seductively easy to stop halfway through the chain and simply fix a symptom, hoping that the problem will go away or that someone else will solve the root problem eventually.

Worse, when you're working fast rather than smart, there's no time to stop for serious feedback. Without feedback you cannot learn from the past. There's never time for post-project reviews because you're off to the next project. There's no time for lost customer audits, because, well, they make us feel bad and there's never a good time, so we don't do them.

Working superficially, without feedback, dooms us to Groundhog Days, where we endlessly repeat mistakes over and over again.

And never really fix them.

4. OBLIVIOUSNESS

The stakes go way up with this next dysfunction.

How self-aware is your organization? Does your organization really understand how it operates? The overwhelming noise of today's work is drowning out employees' ability to think about thinking. The **execution trap** puts a premium on action over introspection.

Oblivious organizations lack a critical second sight, the ability to simultaneously operate the business and observe its operations. Without self-awareness organizations sleepwalk, moving without consciousness. That's dangerous.

When you're operating in the dark, the precise formula your organization uses to create value becomes an impenetrable mystery. Your secret sauce is even a secret to you. Understanding value creation requires deep insight into the enterprise's complex systematic operation. When you don't truly understand how you create value, how can you create more? Without understanding value creation, how can you identify the right metrics or improvements?

Oblivious organizations live in a self-imposed echo chamber. Without feedback, there can be no learning, mistakes get made and remade, and improvement is impossible.

When you're oblivious, you're surrounded by yourself. You inhale your own exhaust because that's all you know.

Obliviousness causes the muddled mess of measurement. Everyone knows measurement is important, that it's essential for monitoring and improving business, processes, and task performance. But few get it right.

Finding the right metrics is hard work. It takes time and insight to understand the systemic operations of a complex organization and to then identify the few key measures that drive value creation. It's difficult to isolate those critical leading and lagging indicators that are most critical to performance. It's much easier to measure gross inputs and outputs than to selectively identify the leading drivers of value.

Oblivious organizations either guess at their process measures or identify many, in the hopes that the right ones will be among them. Or they fall prey to one of the following patterns:

"We measure what we can"

> *or*

"We measure what we can easily measure"

> *or*

"We measure what we can easily measure that makes us look good"

Learning is lost when an organization fails to conduct post-project reviews, lost customer audits, or post-investment accountability assessments. Each of these promises a great opportunity for improvement and avoiding repeat mistakes. But these possibilities are never realized when the organization is oblivious to feedback.

In managing the ongoing tension between Action and Reflection, action wins, hands down, and the result is obliviousness.

Why are traditional organizations so oblivious?

When organizations are asked why they don't do post-project reviews, you might hear one of the following: *"We have no time," "The project team has already dispersed," "We have no methodology," "We're on to the next project,"* or *"The past is past, let it rest."* But if you look again, the absence is bigger than simple process gaps.

Like email and meetings, there's **no clear accountability** for feedback. It's rarely in anyone's job description, and it doesn't fit neatly within existing structures. No one gets promoted for harvesting lessons learned or punished for repeating mistakes. Even introspections usually have no defined process to reuse lessons learned.

Looking even deeper, the absence of feedback is part of a larger set of defensive cultural behaviors, like the three monkeys, "see no evil, hear no evil, speak no evil." So you hear *"If I don't look, I won't see problems, and if I don't see problems, I can't be blamed."* Besides, looking at problems is depressing. So when we actively avoid feedback, it's actually destructive obliviousness. And obliviousness often leads to oblivion.

5. NARCISSISM: LET'S TALK ABOUT ME

While Obliviousness describes a lack organizational self-awareness, Narcissism is about the absence of sentience, the active sensing of the organization's external environment. Both are forms of sensory deprivation, where internal and external data are distant and unperceived.

When an organization struggles with the tension between us and them, inside vs. outside, the internal perspective always wins.

Of course, most organizations don't operate in complete isolation. There are usually departments charged with looking outward and making sense of the activity that surrounds the organization. They're typically housed within marketing—and typically frustrated. One manager of this type of function complained that his unit suffered from a Cassandra Complex. Cassandra, the daughter of Priam, king of Troy, was blessed with the power of true prophecy. She could foretell the future but was also cursed because, although she was always right, no one would ever believe her. The same was true for her unit.

Examine the agendas of your organization's meetings, the contents of your communications, or the conversations in your lunchroom, and you'll see that it's all about us.

Our organizations are isolated citadels surrounded by high walls, keeping us in, and the other out. And these walls are mirrored, so what we see is ourselves.

When a bias for execution over reflection occurs, organizations don't spend nearly enough time deeply thinking about customers and markets. Key word: deeply.

All organizations pay attention to their customers; no one would ever say the opposite. They calculate customer satisfaction. They conduct consumer surveys and measure key interactions. But most likely the questions they ask in surveys and the interactions they measure are ones **they** think are important. They're still standing in their own shoes instead of the customers'; but it's a dance without rhythm, a display of mechanics without empathy.

You can see this bias whenever a vendor tries to bribe a customer to give them a high score. Or when your Uber driver begs for a rating of 5. Manipulating feedback obscures the opportunity for better understanding customers.

It's hard work to develop a deeper understanding of what customers really want and what their unspoken and unmet desires really are. It requires deep empathy to walk in their shoes and look at the world as they see it. And it takes time and thought, both in short supply.

Tracking only your most obvious competitors, the usual suspects, is taking the easy way out. You need time and perseverance to think about where disruptions may come from and to spot their earliest appearances. When you're too busy to actively observe the external world, you get surprised a lot. And market surprises are always bad.

Let's look at a simple example. Say that one of your salespeople happens to hear from a customer that your biggest competitor is about to launch a major new product. Should that happen, who would the salesperson share that important piece of news with? How would that data travel across your organization? How would it be validated or refuted? Where would it be synthesized with other insights about that competitor? Who would be planning a counter-charge?

In many organizations, the answers might be, *"I don't know,"* *"That's a good question; next question,"* or *"It's not my job."* Perhaps your organization has a small competitor-tracking sub-unit buried deep in the marketing department that handles this sort of issue, but if it does, how powerful is its reach? What percent of possibly useful data does it receive?

The truth is that there's data about customers and competitors, demographic changes and geopolitical trends all around you. Your marketplace offers an abundant stew of potential insights. But **if you're not listening, that data has zero value**.

That's why Narcissism is so damaging. Without a formal, data-driven, and disciplined way to observe, understand, and act on data from your marketplace, you're doomed to be reactive. Without sensing, all your surprises will be bad ones.

When the internal overwhelms the external, your potential for disruption grows enormously. As Jeffery Imelt, the CEO of

GE has said, *"We're not smart enough to predict the future, so we have to get better at anticipating and reacting to it more quickly."*

How well is your organization sensing all of the external data that surrounds you?

6. NOW: IMMEDIATE GRATIFICATION

"A revolution is not a bed of roses. A revolution is a struggle to the death between the future and the past."

FIDEL CASTRO

We're prisoners of the present. In your organization, what percentage of your resources is spent on today's work and today's customers versus future work and future customers? No matter what's measured, expenses, hours, capital, or executive attention, the vast majority is undoubtedly spent on today.

In the war between the present and the future, the present is stunningly triumphant.

Look again at your organization. On one hand, you see the Execution Engine. This is the business framework that operates the current organization, drives its everyday processes, and serves its current customers. It's rooted in operational performance. Today's intensity of competition and the demands of current customers require enormous attention and energy. The Engine's goal is short-term success measured by days and weeks. We feed the Execution Engine everything we have.

In comparison, how large is your investment in the Future? This is the sum of resources dedicated to new products and services, staffing for performance improvement projects, training, incentives based on future performance, and the identification and capturing of potential new customers. Whether it's called innovation, reinvention, or transformation, the Future Investment's goal is long-term success. Its time horizon stretches from next year to far into the future.

The war between the Execution Engine and Future Investment is fought on many fronts, but both perspectives are absolutely essential. All healthy organizations must simultaneously run the business and change the business with equal vigor, but that rarely happens. As a result, most traditional organizations are out of balance—with the scales tipped in favor of today. This can be witnessed in these organizations' lack of appetite for transformation, their risk-averse behaviors, and their focus on current, rather than potential, customers.

The most obvious problematic manifestation of Immediate Gratification is the widespread embrace of Continuous Improvement (CI) throughout the traditional business community.

Paradoxically, CI, which purports to be about improvement and organizational change, almost always creates only incremental gains and little real organizational change.

CI is safe, precisely because it changes so little. It stands squarely in the middle of the current model. Its goal is to eliminate waste, and it's not intended to challenge the current design of work, so it ends up creating **Better Sameness** which is a polite way of saying it tweaks but does not transform.

CI changes no organizational boundaries, redistributes no power, or challenges no long-held beliefs. It's a way to change without changing. No organization wants to be seen standing still. So the best way to kill real change is to do just a little. It's safer and cheaper to tinker than transform.

So traditional organizations launch scads of incremental improvement projects, hold frequent Kaizens, gather for scrums, and host other efforts to tune their Execution Engines. And tune they do. Many of these efforts succeed at their intended purpose, taking waste, cost, and time out of today's work.

Although that might seem positive, the cumulative impact of CI is often trivial. That's by design. Very few of these CI projects challenge the fundamentals of The Execution Engine. Because they leave organizational boundaries intact, they reinforce existing silos of power. CI does not radically transform work.

Jabil, the huge contract manufacturer, once explained, "We have over a hundred thousand problem solvers in our organization, who have all been trained in lean Six Sigma. We've had thousands of successful improvement projects, so successful in fact that we're now hitting diminishing returns. There's so little waste left in our processes that our gains are shrinking. To make a big difference we have to step away from incremental change and reimagine our future."

That's what Better Sameness sounds like at the end of its lifespan.

Transformational change is expensive and risky. The benefits can be huge but the timeframes are long. Big projects don't all succeed. Large reengineering efforts can take 2 to 3 years to complete and achieve their ROI. They require big teams who need to be committed for months. Their investments always happen before their benefits, and the resulting organizational change is always painful. Power is shifted as new decision rights and rules push real autonomy closer to customers. Fiefdoms disappear, and silos are demolished. All of this creates active and passive resistance.

Big change means big benefits and big headaches. The organizations that emerge from transformation are different from when they began. They've left ancestor worship behind.

But Immediate Gratification is much more than just about incrementally improving process performance. All the same issues apply to the funding and acceptance of innovation. All employees and executives are citizens of the present, and when a new future is invented, many organizations go through organ rejection.

Think about Kodak. It was clear for years that digital imaging would be the future and chemical-based photography was the past. But it couldn't let go, which spelled doom. Kodak was full of intelligent, well-intended employees, but the organization's devotion to today destroyed its tomorrow.

This imbalance can also be seen in executive compensation, where, for all the talk about balanced scorecards, leaders are paid for current performance and quarterly returns. As a direct consequence, big problems and big opportunities are left for their successors. Traditional organizations incent leaders to be focused on the short term.

Even more problematically, the problem of Immediate Gratification can be seen in the **gutting of training and education budgets**. What a hypocritical joke this cost cutting represents.

Most organization's Value Statements have some version of Dilbert's Greatest Corporate Lie, "People are our Most Important Asset." Yet across the board, HR investments in improving employee capabilities are dramatically shrinking. If employees were truly assets, the way to appreciate the value of that asset would be to invest in them. Instead, training is an easy target for short-term cost reductions. By placing shareholder needs for dividends above employees' needs for skill enhancement, the true face of the organization is revealed. Cutting training is mortgaging the future.

The organization that doesn't invest in their employees is doomed. The bottom line on Immediate Gratification is that organizations are eating their own seed corn and starving their future. It's not sustainable.

When the Execution Engine crowds out Big Change and innovation, everyone loses.

7. LOCALISM

This final dysfunction is the most damaging—and the most intrinsic—to the old industrial model. Localism is the triumph of the parts over the whole, the victory of business units over the enterprise, where fiefdoms rule over the kingdom. It stems from the center's inability to align its parts.

Localism is failed governance; it's a chaotic war between strong silos and weak corporate centers that traps traditional organizations in an inescapable doom loop.

Localism drives massive dis-economies of scale. It's the opposite of synergy. Synergy occurs when the sum of the parts is greater than the whole (when 1+1=3). But look inside most organizations, and 1+1=0. Instead of leveraging scale, industrial-era organizations suffer from sub-optimization everywhere.

How are your standardization efforts going? Are you getting easy compliance to the notion of a single standard benefiting the entire organization? Or does everyone want to do their own thing? If you're like most organizations, standardization brings out the worst in the old model; there's little progress, lots of lip service, minimal compliance, and zero consequences for active disobedience.

Many organizations can't even agree on small things. One very large government organization has been fighting for years about which ketchup to provide their employees. Each part of the organization wants and buys a different type. This may seem like a small matter until you calculate that standardizing on a single type and vendor would yield millions in savings. For ketchup! In other organizations, the same battle occurs over higher-stake issues such as standardized work processes, common software, consistent employee policies, or shared cash management accounts. While standardization isn't always the best approach, noncompliance of the parts often costs billions of dollars to the whole.

When the power of governing processes is weaker than the power of the parts, the result is a set of well-fortified feudal castles governed by strong dukes and duchesses who prioritize for their territories before the central kingdom. The idea of an integrated entity is academic and remote.

It's the tendency of these strong organizational elements to resist change that makes transformation so very difficult. Partnership is tough when you're not true partners. When Localism triumphs, success is declared in business units—not at the enterprise level. Allegiance is at the local level, not to the enterprise.

Why should large organizations with vast resources be so fragile and susceptible to disruption? Why do organizations full of intelligent employees continue to commit dumb dysfunctions?

It's because the center cannot hold, cannot deploy those resources with a unified hand, cannot aim all their weapons at a single common target.

The problem starts with the abject failure of the strategic planning process. Ideally, a strategic plan identifies those few key objectives and actions that are most critical for the enterprise. It narrows the focus and shouts out what's important and what is not. It should integrate the organization's resources together to accomplish mission critical goals.

But mostly it does not.

Over the past 10 years, whenever employees have been asked what their organization's strategy was, the same sad set of answers showed up:

- What strategy?
- Last year plus 6 percent

- I don't know because McKinsey won't tell us

- Huge growth, big profits, delighted customers, happy shareholders, engaged employees, and world domination

- It's a secret

- It's a bunch of inscrutable analytics

- It's 20 different programs and 30 key metrics

- Why would they tell me?

Instead of providing a laser-like shared focus, the strategy process creates more confusion than clarity. It provides no overarching context for measures to cascade down from corporate to units to processes to performers. It sheds no light on which critical projects should be funded and sponsored. It draws a blank on what activities should be terminated to help fund those that are more strategic.

As a direct consequence, fragmentation occurs. No one owns time-suckers like email madness and meeting mania. But the problem is larger than the failure of planning.

A healthy organizational center must force a balance between today and tomorrow to ensure that long-term capabilities are acquired and integrated. It must ensure rigorous compliance to standards that benefit the enterprise—even if they sub-optimize the parts. It must stamp out resistance to change.

A strong center should resolve the three great tensions that exist for all organizations: Us vs. Them, Today vs. Tomorrow, and the Parts vs. The Whole. An intentional balance is needed to harmonize a smart enterprise. Too much internal focus and customers suffer, too much Now-ism and the future is jeopardized, and too little central power causes the ravages of Feudalism.

These seven dysfunctions plague organizations in every sector. Yet few organizations address and repair them. The hidden logic of the traditional model powerfully exerts its influence through executive and front-line worker actions and behaviors. To continue these costly dysfunctions is just plain dumb. A new model is needed.

PART 2: THE SHAPE OF THE SOLUTION

CHAPTER 3
BECOMING A SMART ORGANIZATION:
FROM VICTIM TO VICTOR

The future does not just belong to the fast, the strong, or the lean.

It also belongs to the smart, to the data-driven.

The smart will spin data into gold, capitalizing on the treasure trove that surrounds their organizations. On one side of this data-driven divide will be victors; on the other, victims. Taking full advantage of all this magnificent data represents the single greatest opportunity of our time.

DATA, DATA, EVERYWHERE

The data explosion changes everything.

In *The Inevitable*, Kevin Kelly writes: *"New information is growing at a rate of 66 percent per year, doubling every 18 months."* Cisco predicts that by 2020 there will be 50 billion devices connected to the Internet. These numbers are astounding.

Our world is teeming with data: internal, customer, demographic, structured, and unstructured opportunity. We're drenched by its downpour. Professor Gary King of Harvard states: *"The data flow is growing so quickly that the total accumulation of the past two years—a zettabyte—dwarfs the prior record of human civilization."* As pundits have noted, at this rate we'll soon run out of words to describe the amount of available data. An August 2016 McKinsey article noted that one-half of the world's data was created in the prior ten months.

Yet few organizations capitalize on this bounty. The global

market intelligence firm IDC estimates that less than 0.5 percent of all global data is analyzed in any way. This potential goldmine presents a huge opportunity for smart organizations who can exploit that data and a huge risk for those laggards who linger in the primitive past. More than great products or services, the skilled use of data will separate the winners from the losers.

This vast opportunity can be understood through Say's Law, named after Jean-Baptiste Say, a 19th-century French economist: *"The availability of supply provokes demand."* For example, when potatoes are plentiful, the number of potato recipes grows because the market expands as the prices drop. As computers became cheaper and more widespread, the market inevitably demanded and got more applications.

The availability of massive amounts of data will **provoke** more and more innovative uses of data. The cost of data will plummet and the value will skyrocket. The availability of untold zettabytes will provoke new types of analysis, which will enable new forms of winning. Data mastery will drive market mastery.

But leveraging this abundance requires new organizational models, a smarter model.

YOU CAN'T GET THERE FROM HERE

A hundred years ago, traditional organizations were born into information poverty. The means to acquire, understand, and use data were far off in the future. The traditional organizational model predates computers and is based on the features of a well-oiled **machine**. Stability was baked into the core design. The underlying principle was that tomorrow would look like today, therefore continuity was critical. Everything was permanent and progress would be slow and evolutionary. Caution was not just prudent, but paramount. Today, this mechanical model is incompatible with purposefully exploiting data.

In fact, the very design of traditional organizations was

designed to compensate for the absence of data. Steep hierarchies were needed to sift through information and to elevate decisions to the top of the organizations, where wise executives could make decisions. When accurate data was scarce, only leaders were allowed to receive and use it. Hierarchies act as filtration systems, intended to abstract data rather than enhance it. When information meant power, executives hoarded data and avoided sharing, giving unintended birth to data silos, fracturing objective reality.

But when multiple views of the truth co-exist, subjectivity is the norm. When there's little data, analysis is secondary.

Pervasive risk management, originally designed to limit instability, has metastasized to constrains data innovation. Big organizations with big assets see change as risky and aggressively avoid the new.

Old-fashioned organizations are either blind to today's data bounty or have no disciplined way of using it. As Frank Capek, the CEO of Customer Innovation, observes, *"There's lots and lots of data, but very little sense making."*

Consequently, traditional organizations have a very low Return on Information (ROI) as shown in Exhibit 1. Every dollar ever spent on hardware or software has been invested for one goal and one goal only, to get **better data**, and then to exploit that data to take smarter actions or make better decisions. Trillions of dollars have been spent on this goal. It's the holy grail of business.

Return on Information requires a complex calculation. On one side are obvious costs, including the IT and training budgets, consultant fees, and performance improvement expenses. The formula should also include calculating the hidden costs of all the uncounted meetings that are held to share and analyze data. These investments are then divided by realized improvements in performance.

Exhibit 1: ROI

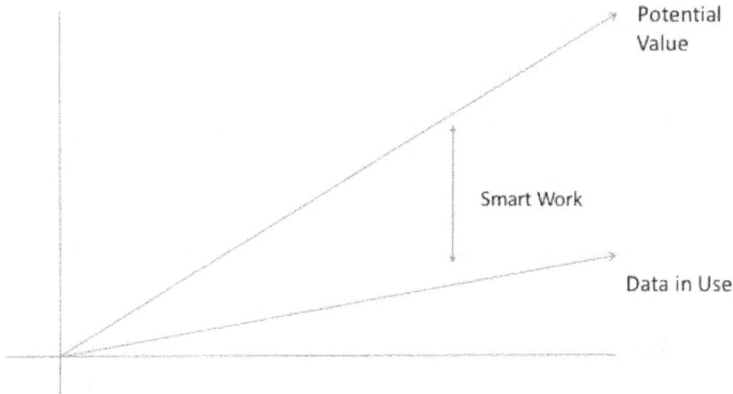

FLYING FROM LINE OF SIGHT TO INSTRUMENTATION

To increase ROI, a new organization is needed, one conceived around information and dedicated to the premise that using information smartly is the best path to value. An organization that can separate the noise from the signal and recognize the difference. One that understands that information required for a decision is good data, extraneous data is not.

In the old model, managers did the filtering based on their limited contexts. The new organization needs both autonomic algorithms to channel that information and skilled front-line humans to use it, especially when judgment or emotional connection is needed.

This new organization's first principle must be that information tells the truth, that it is objective, and allows the organization, in the words of Jack Welch, former CEO of GE, *"To see the world as it is, not as we wish it to be."*

The second principle must be, *"Tomorrow will not be like today, so we must be prepared for uncertainty at all times. Only by being hyper-alert can we survive."*

In this new organization every action yields data and every object is a sensor. When data isn't just a byproduct of transactional work, it's the product itself, where every decision is supported by information and every action is calculated. This requires swapping intuition for information, guesswork for analysis. It requires new ways to navigate in uncertainty.

For amateur pilots, there are two paths to achieve a license. The first is by Line-of-Sight, which allows beginner pilots to fly when the skies are clear in daytime. The second is Instrument Flight Rules (IFR), which requires many more practice hours under a variety of circumstances for licensing. The critical difference is that IFR allows a pilot to fly in more turbulent weather supported by a broad array of navigational and meteorological instruments. This instrumentation greatly augments the pilot's senses by measuring and reporting what can't be directly perceived; IFR is data-driven flight.

Traditional organizations must make the same upgrade, transitioning from flying by line-of-sight to flying with instrumentation. They can no longer simply leverage their senses, intuition, or history. As Steven Haeckel states in the *Adaptive Enterprise*, *"In our unpredictable and volatile world, the past is no guide to the future, trends can be misleading, and surprises are frequent."*

This smart organization needs a new, networked **nervous system** to manage all its data, where technology tendrils link every part of the organization together and where everything must talk to everything else. This never-sleeping nervous system must extend beyond internal boundaries to sense those activities near and far that may impact the organization. It must penetrate deep within the organization to illuminate its own operations with new levels of granularity and precision. And it must integrate that vast amount of stimuli into coherence. It must inhale every type of data and transform that mixture into useful insights.

This nervous system must also feature unprecedented levels of self-awareness and sentience. Enhanced self-awareness will awaken the organization to be consciously aware of its own operations in real time. Conscious organizations need the feedback of measurement to understand how they create value and where waste is located. Sentience illuminates the outside world opening it up to examination and exploration. When organizational boundaries cease serving as mirrors and turn into windows, the world becomes transparent and accessible.

Getting Smart means turning the mechanical model into a vibrant nervous system with a high ROI.

DATA ALCHEMY

Many people think the words "data" and "information" are synonymous. They're not. As Martin Doyle argues convincingly in his B2C article, *"Computers need data while humans need information. While data is raw, information has context."*

Alan Kay, one of the pioneers of personal computing, once said, *"Context is worth 80 IQ points."* Context provides clarification and adds meaning. It adds metadata, data about data. To understand metadata, consider a music CD. Most simply list artists and tracks. When information about composers, performers, or arrangers is added, that's metadata. Context makes information far more valuable than data. It's alchemy, turning dumb bits into smart gold.

The ultimate goal of this transmutation is to get the right data to the right people at the right time in the right format for smart decisions and actions. It doesn't negate intuition or judgment, it informs them. As John Donlon of SiriusDecisions wisely notes, *"Smart Organizations need to collect the dots before they connect the dots."*

That's not the end of data evolution as Exhibit 2 shows. This transformation continues as information and perspective combine to produce actionable knowledge. Perspective provides a purpose; it points the information to a strategic objective. Information without action is inert. Armed with a context and a purpose, knowledge becomes a material asset to be valued. Finally, as knowledge is leavened by experience, the ultimate reward—wisdom—is produced.

Exhibit 2:The Continuum

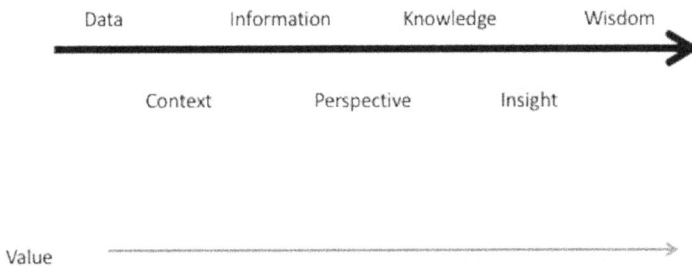

Data	Information	Knowledge	Wisdom
	Context	Perspective	Insight

Value

FROM AVERAGES TO ACTUALS

One reason the data management and analytic constraints of the old organization limited data usage was because of the prevalence of averages. Averages define large numbers well, but do a lousy job on understanding individuals. As a result, their utility is limited. The average human has one testicle and one breast—anatomically interesting, statistically misleading, and absolutely useless.

Consider what happened when Progressive Insurance transformed their averages into actuals. Recently the company introduced a new automobile insurance product called Snapshot. It's a small, innocuous device that fits into most cars' On-Board Diagnostic (OBD-II) port under the dashboard.

The purpose of Snapshot is to monitor driving habits. If you are deemed a safe driver, based on 31 defined criteria, you become eligible for a discount. If your average speed, duration of braking, and normal hours of driving fit Progressive's definition of safe, you save money on your premium.

In the past, Progressive's actuaries sorted through mountains of data to calculate, for example, that a man age A, living on B street, with C driving history, driving D car, was X percent likely to be in an accident, which together yielded a risk level that translated into an insurance price. The premium price was based on the average of all men with those characteristics.

With Snapshot, Progressive can now price insurance based on an individual's unique driving patterns, not on others. The data itself sets the actual premium. This precision was never possible before. It rewards safe driving, which is better for both Progressive and its customers.

Nielsen ratings for television shows, the duration of red and green traffic signals, and medicine dosages have all been based on averages. They're roughly correct but never specifically accurate.

Organizations must transcend estimates and approximations. The data explosion now makes it easier to obtain accurate actuals. Like Progressive, this will make them much smarter and more profitable.

HANSEI OR THE ART OF REFLECTION

Data is but an input to thinking. Alone, it's useless; to create value, Hansei is needed. A central idea within the Toyota Production system, Hansei implies acknowledging one's mistakes and pledging improvement. Loosely translated, it means reflection.

Reflection is at the core of Smart Work. Just as metadata is data about data, reflection is thinking about thinking. Reflection comes from deep, serious thought. It's a disciplined opening of the mind that leads to insight and wisdom.

When organizations are overwhelmed by busyness, reflection is impossible. Serious problems need serious solutions, which can only come from serious thought. Reflection is the antidote to knee-jerk reactions and simplistic solutions. It requires taking the time to mentally process problems and then producing useful insights.

Post-industrial organizations must acknowledge that thinking requires time, that when an employee is staring out into space, he or she is, hopefully, not loafing or shirking but cogitating. Companies must institutionalize time for reflection. Employees need thinking time to achieve mastery of their discipline, to solve complex problems at the root, to learn from their mistakes, and to produce fresh ideas and insights. Smart organizations give explicit permission to think. Even smarter ones demand it.

It takes time to establish a coherent and objective perspective on your marketplace. It takes time to move past superficial views about your customers. It takes time to construct disciplined experiments to test new ideas in the real world. And it takes time to consider and integrate multiple perspectives.

When employees think deeper than their competitors, the organization wins. The insights and wisdom generated by reflection allow organizations to challenge the status quo, to move past conventional wisdom, and generate truly innovative solutions to today's complex problems.

Humility is the proper partner of reflection. It takes courage to say, "I don't know." Too many managers see this as an admission of weakness and fall prey to the myth of executive infallibility. Smart leaders know that not knowing is the only path to true learning.

Finally, an old word with a new meaning makes this all possible. The word is "knowable." For most of history, information was primarily subjective. The world around us was a mystery that yielded little verifiable data. We were guided by our senses, led by intuition, and made decisions based on experiences. We calculated with estimates, not actuals. A few decimals points were all the accuracy we could achieve.

No longer. Individuals and organizations can now easily and inexpensively do what was impossible just a few years ago. Search engines can deliver all the world's knowledge onto your phone. Sensors and other devices capture and send data everywhere. The analog-to-digital evolution has subverted willful ignorance.

At the end of the day, there are only three basic reasons that organizations change. The first is they're in crisis and the choice is change or die. The second is to avoid a future crisis. The last is to seize an opportunity. No matter what your motivation, it's time to get smart.

The opportunity is now. The data you need is here. It's waiting for you. All you need to do is to use it well. That's what Smart Work is all about.

PART 3: GETTING SMARTER

CHAPTER 4
SMART METRICS: FROM GUESSING TO KNOWING

"If you don't know where you're going, any road will take you there."

—THE CHESHIRE CAT

What's your secret sauce?

Do you really know how you create value? Do you understand how a change here affects the outcome over there? Are you measuring the right things, and are you using those measurements correctly?

When you can't answer these questions with confidence, you're operating in the dark. When the mechanics of your business are a mystery to you, effective measurement will be impossible.

Why does this matter? Why should you care? Everyone has measures, but few are comfortable with them. Based on hundreds of conversations, I find that most organizations believe that they have too many or too few metrics, the wrong ones, or they have the right ones but use them poorly.

But smart metrics are a critical key to success; they turn mystery into clarity.

Measurement **quantifies** performance. Measurement translates activities into numbers. It makes meaning out of data. Measurement is how organizations understand themselves.

Measurement is how organizations must navigate the waters of uncertainty. Just as ancient mariners navigated by the stars, smart organizations use their measures as the foundation for actions and decisions.

Measurement is the language of feedback. Without feedback organizations operate in an isolation tank, deprived of sensory stimuli and unable to improve or learn. Feedback is powerful, as drivers have learned when they pass digital signs that display their speed. The display of your actual MPH combined with the speed limit almost always causes a self-correcting slowing.

Without the beautiful arithmetic of measurement, you're in a fast-moving vehicle driving in the dark and hoping for the best. Without measures you have no objective feedback on performance, so there's no data-driven way to improve. Without accurate metrics, you have to rely on history, intuition, memory, or hope—none of which is particularly useful in today's data-rich environment. As Sergeant Friday used to say on the old TV show *Dragnet*, *"We want the facts, ma'am, just the facts."*

MEASUREMENT EXCELLENCE IS TOUGH

Without doubt, measurement is the most conceptually difficult aspect of Smart Work. It takes time and insight to select the right elements to measure, choose the correct metrics for them, calibrate the best performance target, and effectively manage the entire measurement cycle.

One root of the measurement problem lies in the traditional use of measurement as a simple reporting tool. For many, measures amount to an archeological record of history: *"What was our inventory last month?"* or *"What were our sales last quarter?"* The focus on retrospective score keeping, with an emphasis on reporting gross inputs and outputs, meant that what happened in the middle was always a bit of a mystery. But there are many ways to fail at measurement.

FIVE WAYS TO FAIL AT MEASUREMENT

1. "We measure everything"

Today almost every object or action emits data, which means everything can be measured and quantified. With trillions of targets available to be measured, it becomes harder to focus on the few measures that really count. Overload is easy. As reported in *The Boston Globe* (5/17/2016), a new software system at a major Boston hospital that tracks patient care generated so much data that the hospital needed to replace thousands of 12-inch monitors with 24-inch screens to allow the display of all that information.

A major financial services firm in the midst of a large-scale transformation program proudly listed 375 key performance indicators (KPIs) for the enterprise. That hefty number showed everyone how hard their teams had been working.

Quantity can be deceiving. An abundance of measures doesn't drive success, it only reflects confusion and uncertainty. Quantity is never quality, and 375 KPIs is a number that was generated by many compromises and no tradeoffs. It reflects no clear prioritization. The company still cannot identify its 10 most important metrics.

Too many measures spoil the focus. How many performance measures do you have?

2. "We measure the wrong things to four decimal points of accuracy"

In the face of strong negative customer feedback about slow product delivery, a major food company successfully redesigned its new product development process, getting new products to market in significantly shorter times frames. But their major customers were still unhappy.

It turns out that their customers actually valued precision over quickness. They wanted the new products delivered exactly when they needed them, not before and not after. Getting them faster was actually a problem as it caused extra inventory and spoilage. Getting them late was just as bad because precision was needed to align product availability with advertising.

Measures that answer the wrong questions are useless. How confident are you that you have identified the right measures?

3. "We measure whatever makes us look good."

Several years ago, a large industrial company celebrated the achievement of 98 percent on-time delivery to their customers for the third quarter in a row. Everyone in the supply chain felt terrific.

But a deeper look at the on-time data would reveal that the measure was not calculated from the customer's request date, but instead from the company's third revised promised date. And still they only managed 98 percent. If they measured from the customer's perspective, their true on-time rate would have been 53 percent. But that would be depressing, so they changed the measure.

Hiding bad news is a dangerous defensive behavior. As the Toyota Production System states, "Cherish your mistakes." The industrial company denied they had a problem and therefore missed the opportunity to fix it. How many of your measures report in with low numbers?

4. "We measure what's easy to measure"

In 2015, a high-tech industry analyst commented on the fact that a market leader's investment in R&D was one quarter of the investment of its closest competitor. The analyst downgraded the stock, warning that the company would be in trouble as it battled more innovative rivals.

However, the company's R&D numbers didn't reflect the significant innovation that occurred at their suppliers. Because of its scale, the high-tech company was able to demand major innovation from its suppliers as part of its procurement process. They were benefiting from their supplier's ingenuity, but that didn't show up on their financial statements.

Superficial measures will always deceive. Measurement without insight creates misleading information. Have you been lazy about key metrics?

5. "We use 2 percent of what we measure; the rest is CYA"

At a major consumer product company, the operations team held a monthly quality review with its largest vendor. The procurement organization compiled a detailed list of 50 metrics, displayed in Excel, in tiny font size, that they discussed at every meeting.

Half of the meeting time was devoted to all the metrics, without differentiating between the important and less important ones. Notes were taken, and action items were assigned. A visitor would be impressed. However, every meeting repeated the same conversations, the same action items were discussed but never accomplished, and poor performing measures were rarely addressed. At the scheduled time they would adjourn, and then, *Groundhog Day*-style, repeat the exact same process the next month.

When measurement is just an empty ritual, the time spent on them is doubly wasted. How much sleepwalking is part of your measurement system?

SMART MEASUREMENT

The problems with measurement are symptoms of a deeper and more dangerous issue: the insufficient understanding of how our organizations actually work. To derive the right metrics and set the right performance targets, a systematic and disciplined perspective on value creation is required.

To do this, a data-driven framework is needed. This model should cascade from the enterprise's strategy, through the organization's end-to-end processes, and down to performers. The framework links and tightly aligns the enterprise around its strategies, customer requirements, and the needs of other key stakeholders.

Here's a simple way to understand what great measurement looks like. Visualize the cockpit of a commercial jet. You can see hundreds of measurement mechanisms available to the pilots during a flight. But if you ask the pilots what they actively look at, they'll answer that their attention is focused on just a few key measures: speed, fuel, direction, altitude, weather, autopilot status, and perhaps one or two others.

So what are all the other data-providing devices for? They're important when they turn red or beep. In fact, that's when they're critical. This works because pilots (and aircraft designers) deeply understand the systemic operations of their aircraft and can separate the truly critical metrics from the less important. These measures are also balanced to serve all of their key stakeholders: safety for passengers, economic fuel usage for shareholders, and environmental compliance for regulators.

The same pattern can be seen with most primary care physicians. At an annual checkup, they have a standard starter set of metrics, based on your history. Blood pressure, temperature, weight, blood oxygen, etc. They follow up each piece of initial data with questions or additional tests. They, too, have a deep systematic understanding of how the body works. They don't have to measure everything (insurance wouldn't allow that anyway), but they can narrow their focus to look for the current or leading indicators of trouble.

For pilots and physicians, insight is the key. But that takes time and years of practice. Each profession has had decades of experience to hone their craft. But when your workday is full of emails and meetings and work thrown over the cubicle wall, it's impossible to take the hours that are required to deeply understand the systematic operation of your process.

UNDERSTANDING THE TRUE PURPOSES OF MEASUREMENT

The first purpose of measurement is to create **strategic clarity**. A measurement architecture serves as an organizational Rosetta Stone, translating enterprise strategy down into process and performer measures, so that success for the enterprise is defined. This is what Peter Drucker called "the logic of the business." For example, if an enterprise strategy is to grow revenue in China, a supply-chain metric might be to improve on-time delivery in Asia by 20 percent.

The second purpose of measurement is to identify how to **improve business performance**. Rather than historical reporting, measures should illuminate where process improvements can drive business improvements. For example, measures might identify that invoice errors were the primary driver of late payments from customers, which could then be addressed by an improvement project. As one general manager stated, *"If results aren't improving, then you must be measuring the wrong things."*

The third purpose of measurement is to reduce uncertainty through structured **experiments**. Because most organizations are highly complex knots of interdependent work, measures provide a language for constructing hypotheses about outcomes and activities. Smart measurement makes the unknown knowable and the invisible actionable. Consider the following example from *Fortune* magazine (March 2016).

JC Penney had always put men's shoes next to women's

shoes in the women's clothing department, thinking that women would be the likely buyers for their husbands or boy-friends. But Marvin Ellison, JCP's new data-driven CEO thought that this was a terrible idea. So he created an experiment to see if men's shoes would sell faster when placed next to men's suits. They did, and JCP institutionalized that new placement and has seen a double-digit gain in men's shoe sales. *"Pure intuition without any data gets you in trouble,"* he said.

Finally, measurement **communicates what's important**. Smart measurement makes the abstract concrete. It forces alignment around a common target. Think about the United Way thermometer that sits in many corporate headquarters' lobbies. The fact that it receives this prominent placement tells everyone who passes that this effort is important. The scale simply states that it's dollars that are measured and the red area let's everyone know where current performance is. This use of visual information packs a lot of data into one simple sign.

IDENTIFYING THE RIGHT METRICS

The first step in selecting the right measures is to create a model of the enterprise that shows causal relationships. This conceptual diagram depicts how the organization's strategies translate into key metrics. It's a map of the territory taking big goals and breaking them down into clear requirements for units, processes, and people.

The modeling begins with a clear and limited set of high-level strategic objectives and a small number of enterprise KPIs (customer retention, profit/employee, number of percent of revenue from new products, etc.) for each.

The next step involves decomposing those strategies into a cascading chain of causality, an **if/then** set of assump-tions that can be validated or refuted through data collection.

Reading a model upward for example might show:

- if we achieve first-pass resolution of customer-service complaints (individual metric)

- then we will improve customer satisfaction (KPI)

- which will enhance customer retention (strategic objective)

- which will improve profitability because it lowers the cost of customer capture (business goal)

Or a downward logic might show: To serve our enterprise goal of improved profitability, we can reduce net landed costs by 5 percent by consolidating our supplier base.

Each of these examples illuminates possible key metrics. But it's easy to be distracted by what can be easily measured. To narrow down the options, it's important to focus on **controllable** actions. For example, unless you have mind-control capabilities, you cannot make customers buy anything. You can influence them with seductive marketing and assist them with helpful service and available products. Marketing messages, service levels, and product availability are outcomes you can control. Making a customer do anything is beyond your power.

Success requires avoiding superficially easy measures. It's easy to be seduced. For example, what's the right level of employee turnover in your organization? You might answer that if the number is too low, not enough fresh ideas can enter the organization, so the right number might be around 5 percent. You might also say that if the number is too high, it disrupts stability and morale, so about 5 percent sounds right.

Of course there's no right number, or one could take the

consultant's cop-out and say, "it depends." But, quickly responding can only lead you astray, because you'd be answering the
wrong question. Instead of jumping to a knee-jerk answer,
smart measurement requires a bit of thought. Is overall turnover really a strategically critical issue, or is it a surrogate for a
more important concern?

When you think about this, the deeper issue is actually the
retention of high performers. The real issue is organizational
capability. If asked what the right level of turnover of high performers should be, you'd quickly answer as close to zero as
possible. If we flip the question to poor performing employees,
the answer would be clearer as well. This is the value of the
right metric; it answers the right question.

There are a number of clear characteristics of a great metric.

- Strategically aligned/important

- Objective (data driven and replicable)

- Understandable (no abstruse financial acronyms)

- Inexpensive to collect

- Actionable

- Timely

The goal at any organizational level, but particularly at the
process level, is to develop a balanced measurement scorecard comprised of the few vital metrics needed to assess past
performance, current progress, and opportunities for future
improvement. The scorecard must be objective and impartial
to provide useful insights.

The balance of a scorecard is achieved by including both:

- **Lagging** indicators, which tell you where you've been,

such as revenue from new products this past quarter. Lagging indicators help illuminate trends over time.

- **Leading** indicators, which tell you where you're likely to be going. These help you identify problems before they grow, such as identifying a problem in sales forecasting that, if uncorrected could bloat inventory, or opportunities, such as identifying key characteristics in closed sales that allows you to quickly in time to exploit other sales opportunities.

- Many organizations focus on lagging indicators, because they're easier to identify and there are often fewer of them. They also correlate to gross inputs or outputs, which are simpler to count and understand. In most cases, there are many lagging indicators for every leading one, so understanding the difference is critical.

Lagging	Leading
Focus on the past	Useful for the future
Outcomes	In process
Used for reporting	Used for improving
Few	Many
Often not controllable	Always controllable
Example: Sales revenue	Example: Number of leads
Example: Customer satisfaction	Example: on-time delivery

Scorecards must also be balanced among critical stakeholders. In reality, **every metric serves a specific stakeholder**. For example, cost savings serve shareholders because they improve profit while morale levels serve employees because they focus on engagement, compliance metrics serve regulators, and on-time delivery serves customers.

This means that there's an inevitable **tension** within the scorecard. For example, customers certainly want 100 percent perfect orders (delivered as ordered, when requested, complete, in working order, with an accurate invoice). If that were the only supply-chain measure, to get to 100 percent, a company could have infinite inventory, hordes of accountants in accounts receivable, and deliver each order in a limousine. The customers would be deliriously happy, but the company would go out of business, making their shareholders unhappy. Therefore, a cost-per-order measure, serving the shareholder, is needed to mitigate the customer metric. Together they produce balance.

For smart organizations, metric selection requires internal collaboration. For example, a metric of perfect orders forces procurement, manufacturing, logistics, and accounting to all work together for a common goal. Instead of the usual finger pointing and blaming, this measure induces cooperation. A high percentage of perfect orders can only be achieved by all functions working together for the sake of the customer.

USAA, the diversified financial service company that serves armed service personnel and their families, has introduced a smart metric designed to produce collaboration among its diverse business units. In the past, each business unit, such as life insurance or banking, operated independently. If a customer had several transactions, such as questions about car insurance or consumer banking, the customer's call would be transferred from unit to unit for each service need. Today, when customers call USAA, all of their transactions are handled by a single customer service representative who sees the entire USAA/customer file, and when they see a gap in USAA services, will prompt them by saying, "did you know that we also offer...?" USAA wants every dollar that their customers spend on financial services, and the only way they can achieve that is to operate as a single entity instead of a collection of independent units.

These same characteristics are needed for scorecards at all levels from the enterprise to business units, processes, and performers. But there is no end to selecting measures. As the environment changes, as strategies evolve, every scorecard needs to be updated and communicated comprehensively.

SETTING PERFORMANCE TARGETS

In the strategy world, there's a lot of noise about BHAGs (big hairy audacious goals), but once the right key measures are identified, real skill, not consultant clichés, is needed to calibrate the optimum performance target.

It's a Goldilocks situation. The best targets can't be too far or too close to be useful. If the key measure for on-time delivery is too low, it may not motivate your supply-chain performers to overachieve, causing customer dissatisfaction. On the other hand, setting the target too high will demotivate employees or cause them to think that telekinesis is needed to reach their impossible goal.

Critical targeting questions include:

- What do our customers demand?

- What are our competitors providing?

- What are best practices in our industry and beyond?

- What does our strategy require?

The answers to these questions then inform the performance target. Because performance must always be improving, targets change more frequently than key measures.

DEVELOPING AN EFFECTIVE MEASUREMENT CYCLE

Measurement is not an event or an isolated action. It must be a holistic process that includes clear tasks, ownership, and accountabilities. With the right process design, measurement should be a never-ending cycle of data capture, interpretation, and use.

Exhibit 3 below indicates the major steps in this cycle:

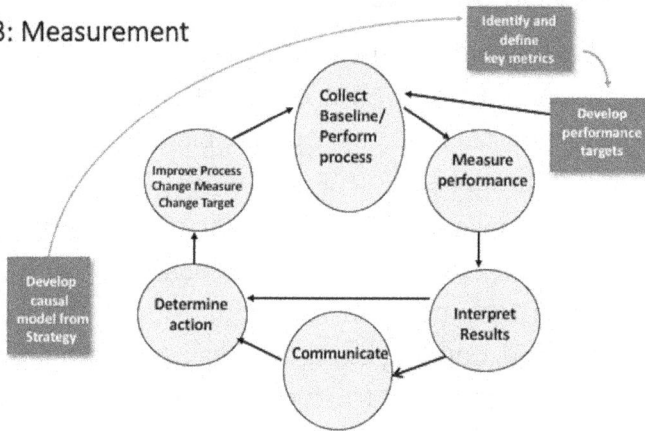

Exhibit 3: Measurement Cycle

Identify and define key metrics

Develop performance targets

Collect Baseline/ Perform process

Measure performance

Improve Process Change Measure Change Target

Develop causal model from Strategy

Determine action

Interpret Results

Communicate

As noted earlier, measurement begins upstream with the articulation of a clear and explicit strategy. That strategy then shapes the causal model, which becomes the framework for a measurement architecture that identifies the scorecard's measures and performance targets. This preliminary work sets the context for the ongoing operational measurement cycle.

To begin effective measurement, a baseline of current performance is needed. The baseline answers the question, *"What is the truth about today?"* Having a baseline allows you, over time, to answer the next critical question, *"Compared to what?"* Without a baseline, numbers have no comparative value.

Once a baseline is established, all that remains is to institutionalize the following iterative cycle:

- Perform work

- Measure the work against performance targets

- Interpret the data

- Identify appropriate action based on interpretation

- Communicate measures and actions to key stakeholders

- Execute improvement action

- Perform work

- Measure again, to see if actions produced the intended result

It's critical to this cycle that each metric has crystal-clear clarity. This means that every metric needs: a definition of the measure, defined data sources, an explicit algorithm that defines the measure's calculation, as well as clear ownership of data collection, analysis, and action. The level of precision also must be defined.

One factor that's often ignored in this cycle is the need to provide value to any group that provides data for measurement. If a team is only a net exporter of data, without receiving any benefit for its effort, it will eventually stop providing good data input.

Another critical step in this process is the effective communication of measures. Visual management is a wonderful tool in this regard. Consider this best practice example shared by consultant Lon Blumenthal:

At a large consumer products company, a business unit general manager (GM) had his staff print out metrics and trend data and placed the printouts on the "metrics wall" near his office. The area where the metrics were posted was about 6 feet high and about 10-to-12 feet across. The wall displayed the results of 25 to 30 measures, including on-time delivery, manufacturing defects, and supplier deliveries. Every morning from 7:30 to 8:00 A.M., the GM would huddle with his key staff around the wall, reviewing the highlights from the day before, and ask various team members to discuss the data. His goal was to align his team on performance, problems, and priorities. By the end of each meeting, everyone was on the same page, and everyone knew the priorities for that day. Every day they repeated this routine. The GM may have owned the wall, but the team owned the actions.

Measurement without communication is silent and useless.

EVOLVING MEASUREMENT

The complexities of measurement will only worsen and the opportunities will grow. As more data-emitting and capturing devices driven by advances such as the Internet of Things (IoT) become prevalent and more information becomes available, choices for measures will grow; focus will be more difficult. It's going to be a target-rich opportunity. Success will go to those who can separate the wheat from the chaff, the critical from the irrelevant, and the differentiated from the commodified.

We will see less manual and far more autonomic measurement, which is data capture that happens without conscious effort. This will cause the boundary between action and counting to blur. Embedded analytics, enabled by in-memory computing advances, will facilitate unprecedented business activity monitoring. Organizations will experience no lag between action and measurement. Just as Google provides search capability while capturing keystroke data, our measurement will mesh with our operation and become one co-mingled activity. Measurement data will course through the organizational nervous system with zero friction.

This will represent both a major challenge and a huge opportunity. As your options expand, all of that information will allow you to know your organization better and better. There will be fewer secrets and mysteries in your work. Measurement will illuminate how we work, create value, and how we can produce even more.

SMART MEASUREMENT SOLUTION SUMMARY

- Start with deep business insight to identify key metrics. Choose only a few.

- Use measurement to translate strategy into action. Then continue the cascade down from units to processes to performers.

- Use measurement as a guide for improvement. If results aren't getting better, you're not measuring the right things.

- Develop a balanced measurement scorecard. Include leading and lagging measures as well as metrics that serve all key stakeholders.

- Experiment with measure until you get it right. Then be prepared to change as the environment changes.

CHAPTER 5
SMART SENSING: FROM INSIDE TO OUTSIDE

Your organization's environment is alive with stimuli. It's saturated with data about customers, competitors, and trends. Every loud beep or faint whisper holds the potential of value for your organization—but only if you can hear and interpret them.

How well are you **listening** for that information, and how well are you **exploiting** it? These are the two primary questions of sensing.

Unless your organization deploys all of its senses intently, it will be surprised by unexpected customer or competitor moves. Unless your organization extends its perceptual awareness outward, it will miss opportunities to better serve its stakeholders. Unless your organization leverages every external interaction as a clue to solving market mysteries, it risks disruption from stealthy competitors.

This isn't news. Every organization conducts customer satisfaction surveys, and most map their customers' purchase journey. But these mechanisms are often conducted from an inside-out perspective: **We** project our internal perspective onto our customers seeking feedback on those services we think are important instead of asking which ones **they** care most about. **We** map **our** touchpoints to them instead of charting **theirs.** We ask, *"How'd we do?"* instead of *"What didn't we do that you really wanted done?"* We ask, *"Was our CSR helpful?"* rather than *"Are we easy to do business with?"*

It's not perspective that must change, it's also proportion. Sensing is often an afterthought, not the main event. To do it well requires a significant investment. When sensing is secondary, it receives limited resources and attention.

Organizations just can't get out of their own way. Narrowly defined metrics, reinforced by our functional perspective, and defined by a set of small tasks, force an *"event perspective"* in customer relationships instead of a holistic one. We fragment the customer interface into transaction-sized bites instead of assessing the entire experience as the customer does. Everywhere we look, we see ourselves.

The objective of smart sensing is to understand **everything** about your customers, which includes not just how your customers are behaving today but how they will behave in the future. And why. It's about using external stimuli as inputs for insight.

When you're doing smart sensing right, you can even sense your customers when they're sensing you. A healthy organization is totally dedicated to its customers. A way to highlight this priority is the acronym TCPAOS, *"The Customer Pays All Our Salaries."*

FAST FASHION

Too many organizations are stumbling around in the dark, blind to the opportunities and dangers that surround them. Market data is now evolving faster than many organizations can capture and exploit it. But this is not true for Zara.

Zara's success is an extraordinary example of smart sensing in action. A unit of the Spanish conglomerate Indetex, Zara has experienced extraordinary growth and profitability over the past five years. Their sense and response innovation has redefined the apparel industry and created a new competitive advantage: Fast Fashion.

Most of Zara's competitors take between nine and 18 months to bring products to market. In an industry based on fast-changing fashion, that's a very long time. Styles came and go more quickly than that. For example, a men's shirt buyer for

Macy's has to predict what colors and collars will be in vogue a year and a half in advance of their arrival on Macys' shelves. The buyers often miss style changes, because they are trying to predict the future, instead of reacting to the market in real time. Inevitably, their guesses are wrong, and to lower their inventory, Macy's has to sell the unsold merchandise down to the secondary market, to stores such as T.J. Maxx or Marshalls, where the shirts are discounted. But you'll never see Zara clothes at T.J. Maxx.

That's because Zara designs, produces, ships, and sells new clothing in 10 days! Zara is so close to the market; they can sell everything they produce without discounting. The company's strategy is to limit production so that there's no remainder inventory to discount and to teach customers that they need to arrive early if they want to buy hot items.

Zara accomplishes all of this through disciplined market sensing. Here's how they do it.

Let's say that on Day 1, a popular pop singer introduces her new video on MTV while wearing a purple blouse. The next day, customers, primarily young women, start asking for similar purple blouses at Zara's stores. That very evening, when all of Zara's store managers gather on a series of conference calls to share what the market is telling them, they identify a strong demand for purple blouses. That evening, Day 2, a decision is made to produce that blouse, and using Zara's high-speed CAD/CAM technology, the garment is designed. Over the next few days, the design is translated into specs that drive cutting, stitching, and dying. Within a week, the product is being shipped.

The purple blouse then shows up on Zara's retail shelves while the singer's video is still in play on MTV. In its market sensing, Zara is both fast and smart. The company exploits real market data without delay, then makes decisions based on that data swiftly, which allows it to capitalize on opportunities in real time rather than waiting and hoping. Because of smart sensing, Zara is just 10 days away from the market, while its competitors are many months away from cashing in on fads or opportunities.

FOCUSING OUTSIDE

While smart metrics help the organization know what's going on inside the organization, there's a parallel need to better understand the external. A smart organization must perceive and understand both its inside and outside.

Simply put, the purpose of this smart sensing is to get ever closer to customers, defeat current and latent competitors, and exploit market trends.

Smart sensing requires perpetual vigilance to hear the faint signals of potential disruption early, before customer unease becomes unstoppable. This environmental scanning is a proactive search for opportunity, a constant scan to find ways to navigate safely amid darkness and turbulence.

This is why smart sensing is so important. Without a formal, data-driven, and disciplined way to observe and assess your environment, you're doomed to be reactive. Without proactive smart sensing, all your surprises will be bad ones. Without funding aggressive external exploration and designing real accountability, you'll be disrupted and out-anticipated. If you're stumbling around in the dark, you'll never achieve first-mover advantage.

Sensing is not unusual behavior. It's what every living organism on earth does to survive. Although every organization performs some sensing, many conduct theirs haphazardly. Here are a few common problems:

Deaf and Dumb—Not Looking Outside: The walls around these organizations are high, thick, and sturdy. Insularity blunts the curiosity that drives marketplace sensing. This is especially true with organizations that embrace a NIH (Not Invented Here) mentality. These organizations have succumbed to the myth of **"We're Different,"** an attitude that the organization is unique and can't learn from the outside. This is deadly: When an organization truly believes that it really is different, what could ever be learned by looking outward?

Denial—Sensing but not Believing: Some organizations do actively explore their environments, but internal disputes negate their findings. Kodak, despite its longstanding reputation in traditional photography, was actually the initial inventor of digital cameras. Due to the constraints of its massive sunk costs in chemical photography, the organization went into denial about the trend to digital. Kodak didn't want to believe that its world would change, so the company chose not to see it.

Delusional—Seeing what isn't there: Several years ago a major bank conducted a customer satisfaction survey with its retail customers. The results showed that 70 percent of the bank's customers were satisfied with its services. The CEO was astounded at these findings because many other data sources, including his personal visits to several locations, had revealed significant customer discontent. So the CEO asked to see the survey instrument itself. To his surprise he saw that customers had been given only three choices for response to the question "*How do you feel about the bank's service*?": *"1) Extremely Satisfied," "2) Very Satisfied,"* and *"3) Satisfied."* In other words, 70 percent of the respondents had given the bank the lowest score possible.

Distracted—Too busy to do it right: Some organizations are so focused on collecting data, they have no time to analyze it. Others get stuck in analysis paralysis and never produce actionable insights. Others only look superficially, relying on historical transactional data.

Despite these problems, the primary barrier to smart

sensing stems from the fact that it doesn't fit neatly into traditional operating models. Some examples of this misfit include:

- Sensing is viewed as tomorrow's work; therefore, it takes time and resources away from today's frantic and overloaded operations

- Sensing is seen as a staff rather than line responsibility, so it can't be very important

- Sensing has no real ownership or accountability attached to the capture, interpretation, and distribution of data

- Sensing rarely has an immediate ROI, because results take time to be meaningful, and impatience wins over substance

When an organization executes smart sensing, real thought is needed to shape the questions that must be answered. The best exploration goes far beyond simple like/dislike touchpoints or happy/sad reactions. Smart sensing must go deeper than quantitative responses to customer satisfaction surveys, net promoter scoring, or simple journey maps. Ask these questions instead:

CUSTOMER QUESTIONS

- Why have we lost customers this year? What were the three biggest causes?

- What are the greatest challenges facing our customers this year? How are we helping them with those challenges?

- What are our customers' biggest unmet needs?

- Is our pathway to our customers expanding or contracting?

- How might we double the value we provide our customers?

- What do our smartest customers think about us?

- How will the balance of power between us and our customers change over the next two years?

- If we went out of business tomorrow, who would our customers turn to? What keeps them from doing that now?

- Are the answers to the above questions different for different customer segments? How granular should our segmentation be next year?

COMPETITOR QUESTIONS

- Which of our competitors is looking at us looking at them? What do they see?

- How clear are our competitors' strategies? How are they planning to out-compete us? What assets do they have that we lack?

- Who might enter our industry soon? Who has the intent? Who has the capability? Who has both?

- What might our next disruptor disrupt?

- What single potential competitor action do we fear the most? How would we respond if this happened?

- Which of our customers have we lost to whom? Do we know why?

LOOKING THROUGH THE JOHARI WINDOW

To answer tough questions like these, you need a method to organize your smart sensing. I suggest that you use the four quadrants of the Johari Window as a way to segment your quest. For many years, I thought that this tool was named for some tribal wisdom found in the depths of a rainforest. However, the truth is more prosaic: it's named for its two creators, Joseph Luft and Harrington Ingham.

The Johari Window, Exhibit 4, can be used for a variety of purposes, from psychotherapy to business planning, but is perfect for defining the approaches to sensing that a smart sensing organization needs.

Exhibit 4: Johari Window

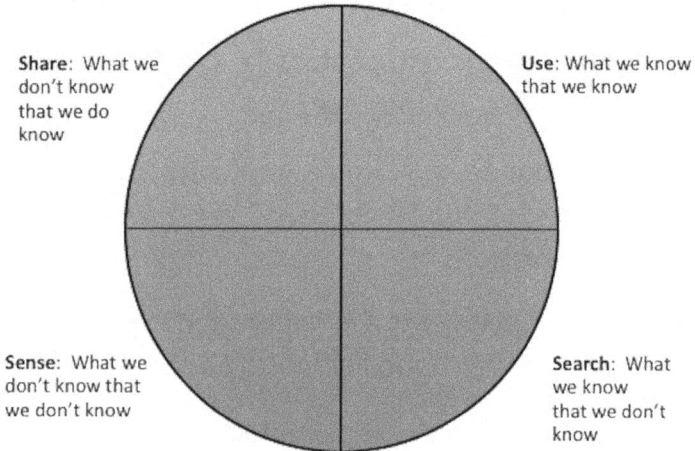

Share: What we don't know that we do know

Use: What we know that we know

Sense: What we don't know that we don't know

Search: What we know that we don't know

In its quadrants we can define four approaches to smart sensing:

1. **What we know that we know**: This is the initial harvest of sensing, the starter inventory of external knowledge.

For example, an organization may know from sensing that a competitor will launch a new product in June. The benefit of that knowledge could be realized by disrupting the competitor's product launch with discounts at key times. The value lies in using data that's already available.

2. **What we know that we don't know**: This is a targeted search, where an organization has defined questions but lacks the answers. This is the easiest sensing, because you already have a preformed question and are looking for a precise answer. For example, you may know that a large customer is looking for a discount, but we don't know how large. The value here is in seeking and finding the answers.

3. **What we don't know that we don't know**: The US military call**s** this the *"Unk Unk,"* the unknown unknown. This quadrant houses the most mysterious and difficult aspects of sensing. In ancient maps, the phrase "Here be Dragons" defined unknown territory. It's tough to search for something you're not aware of and information that has no name.

Too often our **mental** models and preconceptions cloud our searching. We limit ourselves before we begin. It takes both courage and humility to say "I don't know" out loud. This admission is not a statement of ignorance but openness. It's in this quadrant that potential disruptors lurk, hiding just below the surface of our awareness. It's here that unmet customer needs tick like unseen time bombs and that market trends and environmental shifts we're not paying attention to live invisibly. To create value here requires living in the open question, widening the organization's aperture without intentional focus, and relentlessly scouring the marketplace without anticipating easy answers.

4. **What we don't know that we do know**: This is the most frustrating quadrant. It's the unread report about your competitor lying in a dusty file cabinet, the snippet of competitive intelligence overheard but not shared by a salesperson, the terrific improvement idea created in one plant but never communicated to other locations. Value can only be realized by inventorying your data and then managing its sharing.

SENSING STORY

"In the absence of rigorous customer intelligence, companies are left to rely on assumption, history, intuition, or gut feel. None of which have been proven to be reliable engines for continued growth."

—FRANK CAPEK, CEO of Customer Innovations

It's not enough to passively sense the market. The true value of sensing comes from converting market insights into actions that shape the marketplace. Consider Texas Instrument's (TI) calculator business.

In 2015, TI held a dominant 93 percent share of the graphing calculator market in the US. Its base model, the TI-84, had just 480k of ROM and 24kb of RAM, its tiny black and white screen was a mere 96x96 pixels, and it retailed for between $100 and $150. In comparison, Apple's iPod Nano, which sold for $109, came with 16 gigabytes of memory.

How has TI achieved this dominance? Its success came by sensing and shaping the public school mathematics market. Years ago, TI realized that its calculators could be more than replacements for slide rules. By listening to all of its external stakeholders, the company realized that math teachers and math departments in middle and high schools needed help in updating their math curricula. TI stepped in and began assisting in the development of the curricula and teaching plans and embedded its calculators deeply inside the math classes. In many schools now, students' homework assignments show TI calculators and which buttons to push to solve problems.

TI realized that students who actually use the calculators, parents who purchase the calculators, and retailers such as Staples, are only bit players in the math education ecosystem. It's the math teachers who, every September, tell their students which TI-calculator to buy, based on the TI-assisted curricula that are the dominant stakeholder.

The teachers recommend TI because the company has helped solve many of their real-world problems. TI helps with the design of lesson plans and homework assignments. TI maintains a '1-800-TI-CARES' 24-hour telephone hotline, so when students ask their math teacher a tough question, the teacher can call TI that evening, get an answer, and help the student the next morning. The company has hosted more than 100,000 teachers at its Teaching with Technology workshops. It has also endowed professors' chairs at teaching universities to help influence the next generation of math teachers.

Smart sensing is not just about focusing on today's customers, but also on ex-customers and **tomorrow's** customers. It's about understanding the world from the customer's perspective; it's about experiencing deep empathy for their issues and their finances. It's about sincere empathy and achieving a deep understanding about what the customer is trying to accomplish and asking, "How can we help?"

THE LOST CUSTOMER AUDIT

One of the most powerful and rarely used tools of smart sensing is the Lost Customer Audit. Whether you compete in a B2B or B2C world, it's amazing how few organizations take the opportunity to step back and conduct a thorough analysis of why a customer, who once did business with them, stopped handing over money. The loss of a customer should be an extraordinary organizational learning **opportunity**, but when I've asked organizations if they conduct such post-mortems, the answer is almost always *"No!"*

When I ask them why not, I get predictable answers, *"we're too busy"* or *"it's not my job"* or *"I'm too focused on satisfying current clients to think about lost ones."* In addition, this is another orphan task in that no one owns these reviews. There's no tidy home for this activity. Salespeople are too busy and marketers are off to their next program.

Finally, there's the emotional unpleasantness associated with defeat. Thinking about ex-customers makes everyone feel bad, so we, and the organization, avoid this learning opportunity, even though understanding why a customer left you can be the key to keeping other customers from leaving you. What a spectacular opportunity! And what a waste when it's not performed.

Learning from lost customers would certainly help customer retention, and deeper insights can yield market share and upselling opportunities. The Lost Customer Audit, a simple sensing exercise, may be the single best learning opportunity an organization has.

THROW YOUR EXECUTIVES OUT INTO THE MARKEPLACE

Another valuable smart sensing technique involves getting your senior executives out of headquarters and into the marketplace. Too many executives spend all their time hanging out with other senior executives, lunching in the executive dining room, meeting in the executive conference rooms, inhaling each other's exhaust, and engaging in group-think. No wonder so many of them don't really understand how their companies work or what their customers want. It's no longer part of their daily experience. *"Customer"* becomes a conceptual not visceral topic.

Executives see market data that has been abstracted, with smoothed-out scale and geography. As it's moved upward, the data loses detailed granularity and no longer represents a perceptible reality: the marketplace becomes one big spreadsheet. This is a different world than the one experienced by customers, one that can't be simply experienced by emulating TV's *Undercover Boss*.

IBM and Humana, among others, have created disciplined programs to get their senior executives active in the marketplace. The top 40 executives in each company are also active salespeople. They spend time with real customers: listening to them, hearing service complaints, and crafting the case for why their companies are better than the competition. They have to get the sale. This personal experience is far more meaningful than a dry report in helping senior decision makers sense and understand marketplace realities.

Humana has taken this approach even further, requiring that its entire senior cadre spend several hours every month in the complaint department. There's nothing like hearing a distraught mother worried about her child's health and why Humana has been slow to pay a provider's bill, or why a procedure isn't covered to make the market experientially real. Humana takes customer sensing seriously and focuses on four aspects of customer care:

- Know Me

- Show Me you care

- Help Me

- Make it easy for Me

Siemen's Gas Turbine business takes this approach another step further. Its annual report lists the number of days leaders spend with customers; this time is one of every executives key personal metrics.

IN THE CROW'S NEST: DISRUPTOR PARANOIA

Most organizations watch current competitors. It's the normal course of business to learn and steal from peers. But in today's world, that's not nearly enough, it's just table stakes.

It's not crazy to be swiveling your head back and forth constantly scanning for disruptive new competitors; it's crazy if you don't. Who could have predicted Ford worrying about Google in the automotive world, or Marriott being outperformed by Airbnb, or taxi medallions losing 90 percent of their value to Uber's ascendance?

No niche is safe, and no competitive advantage is enduring. Entrenched winners need to actively look at all new market entrants to assess their disruptive potential. Like weeds, seen early enough, disruptors can be identified and uprooted. Once established, they become difficult, if not impossible, to kill. As Andy Grove, former CEO of Intel once wisely advised, *"Only the paranoid survive."*

TRADITIONAL COMPETITOR SENSING: EXTREME VERSION

Think about Coke and Pepsi. How much do you think they know about each other? How detailed is their respective competitive intelligence?

Given their extensive oligopoly, it's no surprise that they're absolutely obsessed with each other. Years ago, when Coke had to withdraw New Coke from the marketplace, Roger Enrico, then CEO of Pepsi USA, gave all Pepsi's employees the following day off and titled his next book, *The Day the Other Guy Blinked*. That's intense. Coke and Pepsi each have detailed organization charts of the other, precise specifications of the other's bottling plants and product formulas, and deep insight into each other's financials.

How deep is your knowledge of your primary or smartest or biggest competitor? How much do you know about their executive team and their predilections? Can you go deep into their unbroken-out financials? Do you know what's in their product pipeline?

Carl Von Clausewitz, the great military strategist who is famous for his quote *"War is the continuation of politics by other means"* also said, *"Judge your adversaries by their capabilities, not what you assume is their intent."* Or, to paraphrase the sergeant in the old TV show *Hill Street Blues*, *"Disrupt them before they disrupt you."*

MARKET SENSING TACTICS FOR CUSTOMER INSIGHT

The better you understand your customer's business, the better you will be able to understand their unmet needs. Here are some ways to actively sense smartly:

- Read their (customers and some suppliers) industry magazines

- Map their Customer Journey with their customers downstream

- Turn your call centers into sensory organs and data-driven listening posts, where a complaint is a signal, a compliment travels widely, and a comment about a competitor is consolidated and distributed

- Make your salespeople responsible for getting and using competitive intelligence
- Craft powerful customer personas and test them
- Attend your customer's industry conferences
- Model your customer's financials to understand how they make and spend money

MARKET SENSING TACTICS FOR COMPETITOR INSIGHTS

- Map their processes and assets
- Leverage their ex-employees
- Build competitive models
- Intuit their strategies
- Question shared customers

ENVIRONMENTAL SENSING

While marketplace sensing is unique to an organization and its context, sensing must also extend beyond the specifics of industry and sector to span the globally connected world. That means spending energy and resources on assessing major trends in demographics and psychographics to better understand future staffing issues. It means paying attention to environmental and climate issues as they relate to products and processes. It means studying geopolitical and macroeconomic patterns as you plan international growth.

THE PROCESS OF SENSING

Regardless of its benefits, smart sensing will never produce value when it's seen as an opportunistic foray, or an event, or a program. For sensing to deliver a stream of value, it must be considered a value-added process. Smart sensing must have an intentional design of its tasks, a clear flow of data and decisions from targeting to data capture, through interpretation, and out to use and exploitation. There must be a business case and an owner who is accountable for its outcomes. This process must be marbled into every customer-touching task and process within the organization, and every employee needs to understand the value of external sensing and their roles and responsibilities within the process.

THE ZEN OF SENSING

- Humility: Your most critical information is the information you don't have yet

- Honesty: Your most important questions are the questions you can't answer now

- Learning: Your biggest discoveries lie in the information you haven't sought and in the questions you haven't asked

SMART SENSING SOLUTION SUMMARY

- Go deep, and listen closely. Your environment is full of potentially useful data.

- Customer empathy is critical. Understand them better than they know themselves.

- Competitor paranoia is rational. Keep vigilant watch for unexpected disruptors.

- Involve leadership in both selling and customer service. This will make the market real for them.

CHAPTER 6
THE IMPERATIVES OF SMART IMPROVEMENT: FROM BETTER SAMENESS TO TRANSFORMATION

75 percent of improvement projects fail.

That's the number most academics and consultants believe is the average failure rate for performance improvement projects. Three out of four don't achieve their promised objective. It's an extraordinary waste of enterprise resources and unintended cause of employee cynicism.

The best way to improve the success rate of improvement projects is to understand why the rate is so low. Here are the ways to improve your success rate, the imperatives of transformation.

KNOCK DOWN YOUR SILOS

What do those hundreds of emails you get and the endless meetings you attend have in common? They are all attempts to connect work across organizational barriers. The emails ask for information, and the meetings connect the dots between different parts of the organization. All that communication and meeting represents the organization frantically trying to put Humpty Dumpty back together again.

Organizational **fragmentation** is the single biggest cause of poor business performance. Fragmentation, the opposite of synergy, occurs when the whole is far less than the sum of the parts and thrives when success is defined locally. When small fiefdoms litter the enterprise, the organization splinters, leading to the triumph of the parts over the whole.

It's organizational **feudalism.**

To better understand the fragmentation within your organization, consider this updating of the fable of the Six Functional Workers and the Order Fulfillment (OF) process:

- One worker looks at OF and says, "It's all about inputs, therefore raw material costs are the key metric."

- The second says, "Inputs are of zero value unless they are moved to where they need to be, therefore logistics is the centerpiece of OF and on-time delivery is the right metric."

- The third says, "Obviously you've never been in a manufacturing plant; that's where all our capital is tied up, so long production runs are critical to achieving low unit costs."

- The fourth says, "You guys are all nuts. Without quality, we're nowhere; just do what I tell you to do, and measure variations."

- The fifth says, "Without a bill we'll never get paid, so invoice accuracy is the best measure."

- The last says, "I'm from Sales, how come none of you bozos said anything about the customer?"

Another way to visualize fragmentation is to think about the span of work that connects you with your customer. From the moment you receive an order to the time that order is fulfilled, how many parts of the organization get involved? How many boundaries must be crossed and how many hand-offs are required? For most organizations, the answer would be at least 10 to 20 different departments. At a large consumer products company, 25 separate functions were involved.

Who in your organization is responsible for integrating all those disparate departments into one seamless whole? Whose job is it to put Humpty Dumpty back together? Your CEO's? No one's? Maybe Exhibit 5, created by Dr. Michael Hammer, can further help you visualize fragmentation.

Exhibit 5 Fragmentation

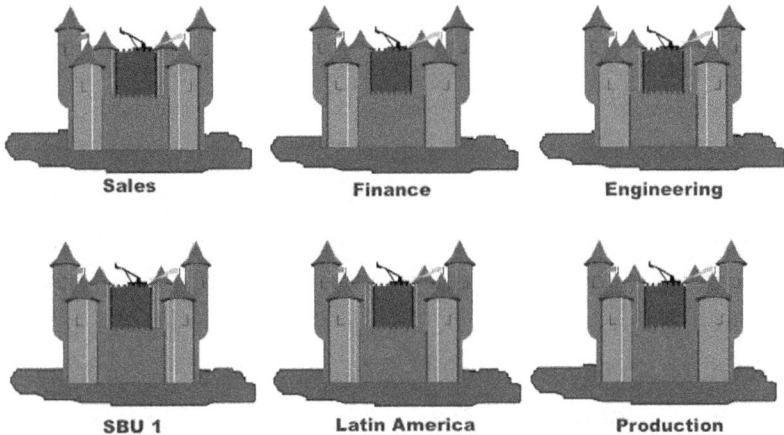

Sales   Finance   Engineering

SBU 1   Latin America   Production

You cannot expect all that royalty to dismantle their own castles. They won't do it; their power, prestige, and pay are derived from their territory. And the castles won't fall down on their own—the foundations are deeply entrenched. You can't take them down brick by brick and hope to finish the demolition in your lifetime. You must knock down those walls—forcefully. As Mao-Zedong once said, *"A revolution is not a tea party."*

Whether you call them silos, stovepipes, smokestacks, or fiefdoms, the business problems caused by fragmentation are enormous. Here are just a few of them:

High costs are generated from the volume of non-value-added work required by multiple handoffs, such as the daisy chain of order fulfillment. Why so many handoffs? The culprits include multiple process versions, non-integrated software systems, different functional metrics, and siloed databases. Costs go up when there are long delays from internal bickering such as when manufacturing focuses on low cost and long production runs while salespeople demand fast turnaround to keep customers happy.

Customer dissatisfaction occurs when organizations show multiple faces to the market or when internal handoffs inflict delays onto customer transactions. As one sales manager explained, *"It's not our customers' fault that we inflict our complexity on them."* Making matters worse, today's customers have been trained by Amazon and Starbucks to expect nearly perfect service all the time. As one CEO of a large chemical company told me, *"If Amazon can get me a $10 book exactly as I ordered in two days, why can't we fulfill our customer's $50,000 order as quickly?"*

Invisible solutions, As Jeff DeWolf of Tetra Pak noted, *"No one can see the real opportunities for* improvement because the walls of our castles are so high. *They're invisible because they live across territorial boundar*ies." In this fragmented world, sponsorship for transformational projects is nearly impossible because there's never just one executive responsible for an end-to-end process. That means that committees of competing executives are required to support and sponsor a project. But a prince who sponsors an improvement project will never allow that project to demolish his castle. And because of data silos, there's no single source of truth to align around.

Here's an excellent example of how transformational process redesign defeated organizational fragmentation.

In 2014, Tyson's Food Service business was having a serious problem with its ability to change product prices quickly in the face of market opportunity. When Tyson was charging $25 for a case of Product X but could gain significant additional sales volume if they dropped the price to $20/case, it would take the company anywhere from 3 to 21 days to align on a new price. As a result, Tyson was losing sales to smaller, more agile competitors who were able to discount quicker.

Why was it taking Tyson so long? At the time, Product X was offered by three different internal Tyson business units, and each unit wanted both the profit margin and the volume associated with any sale. As a consequence, they were bidding against one another for the customer's business. The back-and-forth bidding was where all the time was spent.

Resolution was achieved by strong leadership and an open acknowledgment that this situation was a big problem that needed a big solution. A process redesign team was assembled and focused on the pricing problem.

After months of diagnostic work, the team recommended that a process integration capability be created. This capability would be housed in a new group, the Business Integration team, that would be charged with representing the Voice of the Customer and understanding how each product was positioned in the marketplace, independent of business segment. This new group was then given the responsibility for pricing decisions that were based on agree-upon thresholds from the three operating units. They were also given responsibility for amassing competitor intelligence, so that they could model competitor's buying power as a better way to inform competitive pricing.

With explicit and clear decision rights, pricing rules, and aligned roles, Tyson is now making similar pricing decisions within 48 hours. That's an enormous improvement and this has dramatically improved the profitability of the Food Service business.

Tyson's process improvement project is a rare example of transformational change. Most organizations attack fragmentation with minor solutions. That's like attacking a shark with a butter knife. It's a deadly mismatch, and it doesn't work. That's why big change is needed.

EMBRACE TRANSFORMATIONAL CHANGE

It's an unfair fight because the prevailing toolset doesn't match up well against the problem. Today's most popular improvement approach is Lean Six Sigma, which is a hybrid of Toyota's Production System and statistical analysis borrowed from the Six Sigma tradition. Lean Six Sigma is an example of bottoms-up improvement methodology, which means it's generally targeted at smaller chunks of work that are executed at lower levels of the organization. Rather than attacking the entire supply chain in a single top-down project, a traditional Lean Six Sigma approach would be to approach the problem through a host of smaller projects. The goal of all those Lean Six Sigma projects would be improve workflow and eliminate waste.

Who could argue with that? Because it works, almost all large organizations today have bundled their bottoms-up improvement efforts into overarching programs, called either Continuous Improvement (CI) or Operational Excellence (OpEx).

No matter what they're called, however, these programs almost always produce the exact opposite of their stated intentions.

It's a paradox. Continuous Improvement Programs, which are intended to produce improved performance, almost always create only incremental performance gains and generate little real organizational change. They don't change the work as much as they tune and refine it. It's evolution, not revolution.

But there's a bit of a con game involved here. Despite the best intentions and skills of its practitioners, CI often preserves the status quo.

To those who don't want to change, CI is safe, precisely because it changes so little. CI projects operate within the prevailing paradigm and tweak the existing design. Improvement comes from doing today's work faster and cheaper.

But when a process is fundamentally broken, the marketplace has dramatically changed, or customer expectations have radically altered, simply modifying today's work is worse than useless since CI projects gobble up the resources needed to drive transformational change. The illusion of attending to operational problems is merely self-protection.

Lean Six Sigma was never intended to challenge the current design of work, but it does create **Better Sameness,** which is a polite way of saying it rearranges the deck chairs on the Titanic.

Think about the Continuous Improvement programs in your organization. How much deep change have they generated? Have they changed organizational boundaries, redistributed power, or challenged long-held beliefs? For most, they tune but don't transform. CI is a way to change without changing. It's safer and cheaper to tinker than transform. CI is a brilliant defensive behavior.

Traditional organizations launch scads of incremental improvement projects, hold frequent Kaizens, gather for scrums, and host other efforts to tweak their Execution Engines. Many of these efforts succeed at their intended purpose, taking waste, cost, and time out of today's work. But too often, small change simply isn't enough.

It doesn't matter if this incrementalism is driven by fears of Wall Street's reaction to quarterly results, activist investors, sheer inertia, short-term executive compensation, or fear of the unknown. Yesterday's designs still triumph over today's needs.

Stepping further back, the deeper problem is neither Continuous Improvement nor Lean Six Sigma—it's the limited toolset and mindset that organizations deploy to improve performance. When all you have is Lean Six Sigma, everything looks like potential waste. When all change is part of Continuous Improvement, there's no room for discontinuous transformation.

To be clear, this is not perpetrated by Lean Six Sigma practitioners. In my experience, they're a dedicated group of improvers doing their best to help their organizations or clients. Process engineers truly operate with sincerity and great intentions. It's not their fault.

A major financial services company realized this limitation too late. Their well-trained, experienced cadre of internal consultants had mastered statistical analysis, earned many-colored belts, and were proficient in Lean methodologies. These capabilities had served them and their company well. But suddenly, as they approached a major merger, their improvement needs changed. The new projects focused on silos that required demolition, and boundaries that had to change. But these new types of projects no longer fit their bottoms-up training. Their tools and experiences were inadequate to this challenge, so they rushed into on-the-job training and hired a major consulting firm to assist. But their efforts were wasted because the skills and thinking styles needed for transformational change are very different than for incremental improvement.

The company needed out-of-the-box thinking to integrate their castles and major change management skills to deal with anticipated resistance. Neither of these skills fit the profiles of their consultants. They could learn the steps of big change, but they couldn't master them.

Not surprisingly, most of the projects they led failed. It wasn't the practitioners' fault; they were trained in X but asked to succeed at Y. The company's external consultants had the right project skills and methodologies but not the context. They could plan but didn't know the industry or the personalities of the organization. Nor were they skilled at change management. As a result, their projects also failed. The company was left with no return on their big investment in improvement. The persistence of the past, and the organization's limited perspective on change, doomed its reinvention.

The financial services company is not alone. No one asks for big change unless they have to. The time for big organizations to accept that they need this is here and now, as the following story illustrates.

Years ago, CardX, a major credit card company, was having a customer service problem. It was taking 14 days to replace a customer's lost or stolen credit card, while its competitors were replacing cards in a week.

CardX's CEO called a senior team meeting to brainstorm solutions. He began by asking, *"How can we go faster?"* After an uncomfortable silence, one exec said he could shave 30 minutes off the time by eliminating one quality check. Another volunteered a savings of 15 minutes by cutting a second mailing address check. After a tense 4-hour meeting, the CEO succeeded in shrinking the time from 14 days to 13 days and 2 hours.

The next week, this full-page announcement ran in national newspapers: "In six months, CardX is proud to announce a six-day turnaround of lost or stolen credit cards."

What do you think happened in six months?

If you guessed that the new cycle time was six days, you'd be correct. But how did that happen? How could a team of CardX process redesigners take eight days out of the process, when the leadership meeting had found a mere 6 hours? What changed?

Everything. In the CEO's meeting, the question, *"How can we go faster?"* was heard by his executives as, *"How can we do what we do today faster?"* This put the senior team standing squarely in the current process design looking to accelerate the existing way of working.

After the newspaper announcement, the real question emerged. The redesign team asked itself: "What possible ways-can we invent to process a card return in six days?" They began by throwing away the old model, with all its constraining assumptions, and started from scratch. No amount of tweaking or amphetamines could ever cut the cycle time in half. The team realized that only a radical change could do that. That fresh approach quickly yielded several assumption-breaking redesign ideas that solved CardX's problem.

Business Reengineering, as originally defined by Dr. Michael Hammer and Jim Champy, arose from the needs of large American organizations to overcome Japanese competition in the 1990s. Because many Japanese corporations had embraced Total Quality Management far earlier, they were winning in sector after sector. Reengineering was a new approach intended to help American companies leapfrog that competitive disadvantage by creating dramatic process improvements that produced order-of-magnitude benefits.

One primary impetus for transformation today is the threat of disruption. It's small crafty innovators that pose the greatest threat to large industrial-era organizations. Disruptors whose DNA is fundamentally different from traditional organizations and who operate without the weight of history are reshaping the competitive landscape. These disruptors are not using new technologies just to do what traditional organizations do a little faster or cheaper. They're radically redefining and transforming the work. When Quicken Loans can approve a mortgage in one hour while it takes a traditional bank one month, that's not better sameness, it's discontinuous change.

If large organizations want to survive the disruptor onslaught, they need to gain proficiency in all the cells in the matrix displayed in Exhibit 6. This is especially true about transformational projects where there's less experience but more need.

This Exhibit depicts the map of all possible performance improvements. The vertical axis defines the type of improvement. No matter what methodology an organization uses, there are only three essential types of benefits. They're listed below in ascending order of potential value, magnitude of change, and level of difficulty.

1. EFFICIENCY: This benefit refers to getting work done **faster or cheaper.** Lowering the cost of filling an order, or answering a customer telephone call after two rings instead of five, are examples of efficiency benefits. Efficiency is the ratio of inputs to outputs and changes no organizational boundaries or power structures. Such improvements only change the task and not the context.

2. EFFECTIVENESS: The definition for this benefit revolves around **better quality.** When a single customer service rep can answer all of a customer's questions, or when a salesperson is supported by online tools that help adjust prices in real-time, these are effectiveness benefits. Effectiveness can be achieved by driving out variation or through using data to improve decision making. The outcomes have improved while the work is still recognizable. The benefit is an improvement on the current way of working, not a different way of working. Both the task, and some of the context, are changed.

3. TRANSFORMATION: These benefits are achieved from working **differently**. Instead of modifying work, the basic paradigm is altered. Instead of starting with the current process and asking, *"How can we do what we do today*

faster or cheaper or better?" transformation requires that a different question be asked: *"If we were starting up today, how would we do this work?"* Transformation is an escape from the prison of the installed base. When Rich Products replaced its slow, linear, and siloed process design for new product development with a rapid-cycle cross-functional team, that was an example of transformation. When electric utilities replaced meter readers with automated power meters that directly transmitted the customer's kilowatts used and combined that with usage reports and suggestions for energy conservation, that was also transformation.

The horizontal axis of the matrix depicts how much, and which part, of the organization will be affected by the performance change. It ranges from tiny individual steps to large inter-organizational connections.

Task: refers to an individual activity such as entering an order.

Sub-process: is a set of linked tasks such as purchasing raw materials, which includes tasks such as vendor selection and cutting a purchase order.

End-to-End Process: a group of sub-processes such as the supply chain, which might include procurement, manufacturing, and logistics.

Enterprise: all end-to-end processes within an organization.

Eco-System: a constellation of interconnected enterprises, such as an automotive manufacturer and its primary suppliers and dealers.

As this matrix illustrates, there are multiple targets for improvement. Each target requires a different set of tools. As a rule, projects become longer and more difficult, while benefits grow, as they move from efficiency to transformation or from task to ecosystem in scope and scale.

Exhibit 6: The Domains of Change

	Task	Sub-Process	E2E Process	Enterprise	Eco-System
Efficiency		Continuous Improvement			
Effectiveness					
Transformation			Business Reengineering		

Recent research reports have revealed a puzzling mystery. Despite decades of major spending on information technology (IT), American productivity has not improved as expected. The roster of promising new technologies is breathtaking, including advances in Artificial Intelligence (AI), mobile, social, cloud services, big data and analytics, sensors, and the Internet of Things.

In 2015, the International Data Corp. (IDC) estimated that $727 billion was spent on IT in the US. Despite that massive investment, economists have not witnessed the major productivity bump that was included in all those business cases. Possible explanations for the difference in expectations include:

- Frivolity: Workers have been spending too much time on Facebook, Twitter, and games and not using new technologies on their jobs

- Maturity: It's too early in the life cycle of many new technologies for value generation

- Over-Hyped: The promised improvements were over-sold in the first place, and the new technologies just aren't as powerful as their vendors claimed

These may be completely or partially true, but there's an alternative hypothesis that has less to do with IT and more to do with timidity in process innovation and redesign.

Productivity gains will always be limited when new technologies are attached to old ways of working and deployed in support of existing power structures. For example, using AI to automate a 20-year-old process design for order entry is like attaching a motor to a horse and expecting the performance of an automobile. Using an iPhone app to do exactly what a traditional SAP system would do is redundant and expensive folly.

In the technology world, we've repeatedly seen the "less" phenomena. Radio was *wireless*, cars were *horseless* carriages, and early ATMs were *teller-less* windows. We tend to see the new through the lens of the old.

That's what most organizations have been doing with all of today's spectacular technologies. They've been making bigger candles rather than inventing the light bulb. In organization after organization, great technology has been applied to mundane and incremental uses. The past shapes the future as organizational timidity constrains the potential of technology.

The only way to achieve discontinuous jumps in productivity is through transforming work. Consider Exhibit 7:

Exhibit 7: The Shapes of Change

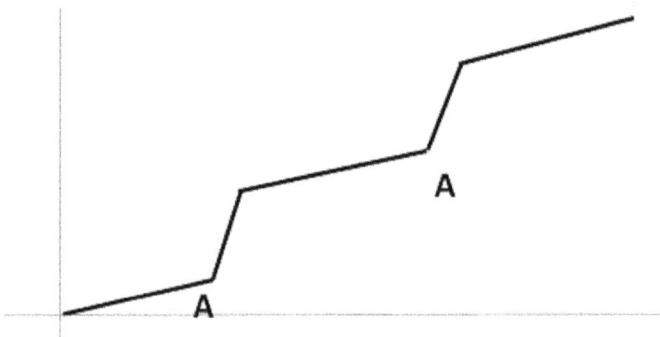

This graph depicts the winning high jump height at the Olympics since 1900. As the graph shows, the winner for many years jumped just a bit higher that his predecessor. But twice, at the points labeled "A," the winning jump showed a dramatic improvement—not just a little better, a whole lot better.

What can you attribute this rapid change to? If you were a track and field expert, you'd know that these discontinuous improvements occurred when innovators came up with new ways to get over the bar, such as the Fosbery Flop where the high jumper actually goes over backwards. *"What lunacy!,"* traditionalists must have shouted when Dick Fosbury introduced his move. But it worked, and it was transformational.

This graph can also represent the productivity gains made possible by integrating new technologies with radical process change. When these two elements are combined, the productivity promise is solved and the paradox eliminated.

DO FEWER BUT BETTER PROJECTS

Performance improvement is never free, but many organizations behave as if it is. Every single improvement project has real costs. Some are easily visible—such as project team headcount and direct expenses—but others are invisible, such as team members' opportunity costs, the lost time of failed projects, or the downstream resistance that delays benefit.

Because few organizations actually measure and track these invisible costs, improvement looks free at both the individual and aggregate level. This cost is unowned. It doesn't live in any one manager's P&L, except the CEO's. So when it looks like they're getting something for nothing, management actively splurges on improvement. Projects galore for all!

Compounding the problem, every organization has a finite capacity for change. This is rarely acknowledged and hardly ever measured. This capacity is shaped in two dimensions, the first of which is staffing.

Somewhere, there's a real number that captures the available time of all potential project team members and all possible consultants. It's a big number, but it's not infinite and it is real. It's also invisible, so no organization ever measures this staffing capacity limitation. The capacity limitation is also realized in the number of available project managers an organization can field. There are also limits to the number of projects that can be coordinated effectively.

Secondly, there are real limits to how much change an organization and individual employees can absorb. Employees are not porous sponges capable of soaking in infinite new ways of working.

Change saturation is real. You see it when employees start talking about "change fatigue," as wave after wave of projects causes them to learn, unlearn, relearn, skill, and reskill, and execute new screens, new tools, new scripts, and new patterns of work. In their zeal for improvement, organizations neglect to add time for internalization of change. In their search for agility, they allow no time for employees to achieve mastery before they must change again. All of these limits are also rarely measured. And so many organizations don't recognize their existence. They behave as if change capacity is infinite.

The result is an orgy of change projects. Organizations gleefully launch thousands of programs and projects, most of them doomed to fail.

This is **Project-itis**, the malady mentioned in Chapter 1. When there are too many projects, staffing capacity is stretched beyond its limits. Many teams are poorly staffed in terms of both time and skills.

When team members are assigned to projects for only 5 to 10 percent of their time, intensity and focus suffer. Scheduling team meetings becomes a nightmare, and the project drags on and on with little momentum. Staffing becomes a crapshoot. When there are more projects than great project managers, there will be failures of planning and leadership.

With an excess of disconnected projects, prioritization and integration become mathematically impossible.

The remedy? It's simple and clear—but difficult to do: Just Say No! Shout Hell No, and everyone will hear it. Saying No! loudly and often will begin to reduce the number of efforts. Even better, say Stop! Just because a project began doesn't guarantee it immortality. If it's in trouble, delayed, redundant, or problematic, just end it and send the team members back to their day jobs.

When there are fewer projects, team members can better allocate their time, which will improve their skin-in-the-game and identification with the project. Scheduling will be easier, and the project can be completed sooner.

With fewer projects, the organization can put its best managers on the most strategic ones. Project Managers can be assigned to the projects that best suit their experiences and capabilities.

When an organization is fighting too many wars, it's impossible to win all of them. Resources are spread too thinly and concentration is scattered. The same is true when waging change.

The second leading cause of project failure is that organizations are so busy executing change there's little time left for **learning** what works and what doesn't.

In your organization, what's **your** project success rate? Do you know? And if not, why don't you know?

If yours is like most organizations, success rates aren't measured or tracked. Poof! The project ends, the team dissolves, and new assignments start all over again. It's an endless cycle devoid of introspection and learning. Alternatively, the nature of success is redefined, and then redefined again. That way, everyone can be a winner, even if the project never delivers any value at all. It's pure sophistry. Or projects simply never end, so they can't be called failures. Every organization has hordes of zombie projects like this, projects that are dead but don't know it.

This failure of conducting project post-mortems is also a strongly defensive behavior. It's really depressing to fail most of the time, and if the number isn't visible, it doesn't have to be acknowledged. So success isn't measured. Besides, the measurement of project success is another organizational orphan.

It's actually worse than this. Most organizations don't even conduct post-project reviews to learn from their success and failures, which means that learning doesn't occur but repeat mistakes always do.

One organization that takes this learning seriously is the US military, where the post-project post-mortem is called the After Action Review (AAR), or sometimes the Hot Wash. The typical AAR focuses on the following five questions:

1. What went well? AARs always start with the positive. This makes it easier to address the problems.

2. What could have gone better? The worst thing that can happen is to hide a problem. When it's invisible, it can't be corrected. AARs are designed to make it safe to acknowledge problems and bring them to light so they can be addressed.

3. What did we expect to happen? In every tactical situation, there's an expected and explicit scenario thought out in advance, with the hope of eliminating surprises.

4. What actually did happen and why was it different from our expectations? This critical part of the dialogue

compares reality to the anticipated scenario to probe why they were different.

5. What did we learn, and who else needs to know it? This ensures that learning is gained and distributed. It's insight harvesting with the goal of ensuring that mistakes don't recur.

When this type of learning happens on a routine basis, repeat mistakes disappear and projects get better. And better is better.

DIGITIZE YOUR PROCESSES

If you work at a large industrial-era organization, your processes were born in an age of information poverty. Because they're relics of the Machine Age, your process designs can't easily exploit new technologies or take advantage of today's data-rich environment. When mapped or modeled, your processes depict tasks and physical movements instead of decisions and information flows.

We now live with **information abundance**. There's data, data everywhere, and our processes need to be fundamentally redesigned to capture and use all that information to achieve high performance.

To repeat an unexpected truth, every single dollar every organization has ever spent on hardware or software has actually been for one singular goal, the collection and use of good data. Computers and systems are merely means to an end, never the end itself. All technology allows us to do is generate, capture, and use data.

When organizations attempt to graft new technologies onto antiquated processes, it's like motorizing a raft. The outcome is sub-optimized, and the investment is wasted. Instead of improved performance they get fossilized processes frozen in software. What good is accurate real-time data if an emergency shipment to a customer still needs three supervisory approvals or a customer service rep still needs to ask a supervisor for permission to issue a small credit to a waiting customer.

Every organization must now address the shrinking half-life of process designs. In the past, a well-designed process could last for 5-10 years without needing a fundamental redesign. But today's turbulence has ended that stability, and as the environment is changing frequently, so must process designs.

Behind all this change is the extraordinary explosion of information technologies. Once there was a slow curve to technological maturity, but no longer. For perspective, in 2015 there were 104,000 YouTube videos streamed every second of every day. Even more extreme, the global IT service firm Huawei estimates that by 2025, 100 billion people and things will be connected to the Internet. Everything will be wired; everything will emit, capture, and use data.

Processes must be reconceived to take into account that every movement will generate data, every object will have a sensor, and every process decision can be supported by data and measured in real time.

None of this was ever possible before.

Both process design and execution are now all about the data, as Hershey learned when it placed chocolate next to marshmallows in its retail planograms and sales of both rose (as any lover of s'mores could have predicted).

In the 1970s Walter Wriston, the CEO of Citibank, proclaimed, "Information about money is now more valuable than the money itself." The same is now true about processes.

That's why organizations need to digitize their processes. But what does that mean? What's a digital process and how would you recognize one if you met it on the street?

Here are the primary characteristics of a digital process:

- From a distance, the process would pass a Turing Test, meaning that an observer couldn't tell which tasks were done by man and which by machine.

- Immediacy, availability, granularity, utility, transparency all dramatically improve.

- The simplest tasks within the process would become **autonomic**, that is they would require no conscious action, creating what Doug Drolett of Shell calls a *"touchless"* process. This might happen when a truck finishing a delivery would automatically send a "delivered" signal, as well as trigger the sending of an invoice.

- The process would operate using actual data, not averages—the way that Progressive's Snapshot chip senses a customer's driving patterns and prices their policy based on that person's specific driving skills, not on individuals like them. Other ways that actuals could replace averages might include: turning highway tollbooths into a speeding ticket machines, charging airline passengers differing fares based upon their luggage and body weight, or connecting thermostats to vending machines so that prices could rise on hot days. Actual data makes all of this possible.

- Measurement and execution would be simultaneous and interconnected, the way that Google connects and counts within a single action. This would drive a process's ability to be self-correcting. As the process continually scans its inputs, outputs, and constraints, it could add capacity whenever needed—the way the Singapore's Metro system adds cars and stations at times of peak usage. A utility's smart grid operates the same self-correcting way.

- The tasks with the process would be both inter-organizational and disintermediated, in that sub-processes might be created or operated by different organizations seamlessly. This would take plug and play to the extreme.

- The process would be proactive and predictive. For example, if an online shopper buys hot dogs, the process may produce a prompt that suggests that they may also want buns, relish, onions, beer, and diapers.

- Its core would be composed of a data-driven algorithm as today's airline seat pricing process is.

Pushing further, my colleague Brad Power argues, *"When you digitize a process, you get big data; when you get big data, you can do machine learning; when you have machine learning, the system can get very smart on its own and continuously improve without much data scientist involvement. And when you digitize a process, it becomes software and when something is in software, it has wonderful properties such as 24/7 availability, low cost, consistency, reliability, and easy continuous improvement."*

MAKE DATA-DRIVEN DECISIONS

If the value of all hardware and software investments is realized by using good data, then the value of all data can only be realized around making good decisions.

A decision is data in action. Good decision making requires getting the right data at the right time to the right individual in the right form to be useful. This means that data quality becomes paramount. In a digital process, data is not just the by-product of a transactional process, it's the goal itself.

It also means that organizations can define a digital process as a set of decisions that link together to create an outcome of value for a key stakeholder.

Process engineers of every stripe will need to learn how to deconstruct and model the anatomy of decisions: the suppliers of data and options; the inputs needed such as data and tools; the process of decision making, including the algorithms; and the decision outputs.

A focus on tasks dominates process archeology because action represents the most visible element of the Machine Age. Tomorrow will be all about data and decisions. In the future, we'll care less about functional handoffs and more about data flows and decision rules.

The future belongs to those who use smart data to make smart decisions.

SMART IMPROVEMENT SOLUTION SUMMARY

- Knock down your silos to create high-performing processes. Fragmentation is the enemy of performance.

- Avoid the trap of better sameness by launching bolder transformation projects. Incremental improvement will always hit diminishing returns.

- Do fewer but better projects for a higher success rate. This will help staffing and alignment.

- Digitize your processes to escape old design limits. Old process design will always limit the value of new technologies.

- Develop data-driven decision making deep into the organization. Ensure that there's a shared objective reality in the organization.

CHAPTER 7
SMARTER WORKERS: FROM TAYLOR TO TOMORROW

Smart organizations need smart employees. They need workers who are motivated, capable, and prepared to do whatever it takes to help their organization succeed.

That's a tall order. Gallup reports that in 2015 only 32 percent of American workers were "engaged." They define engagement as involved and enthusiastic about their jobs. That rate has not changed over the last 5 years. It's a complex problem with multiple causes.

Part of the engagement problem stems from the dramatic changes in workers' relationship to their organization. Long gone is the old contract of jobs for life in exchange for company loyalty. No one has career security, and everyone today is a free agent.

However, while the contract has changed, the basic definitions of worker and manager roles has not. Traditional organizations still cling to old assumptions about power and autonomy, and these antiquated assumptions increasingly frustrate and alienate employees.

Generational patterns are also challenging long-held assumptions about the nature of jobs in today's "gig economy," where everyone is a free agent. Years of downsizing have removed any vestige of job security as more workers hold multiple part-time jobs. As such, the traditional contract between employee and employer has changed. HR policies have yet to catch up contemporary trends.

Finally, the pace of workplace automation, **the robot in the**

room, is upending the world of work. Technology eliminates jobs, a reality that gets more evident every minute. No one and no job is immune. As a manager from the Ontario Teachers' Pension Plan once put it, *"Knowledge work is everything we haven't automated yet."* No one really knows how pervasive this manifest destiny is or how quickly it will proceed.

No matter what, most jobs are not disappearing tomorrow. Organizations will still need humans, perhaps not as many and perhaps not doing the same work, but escalating automation will inevitably commoditize most work processes. Organizations that aggressively optimize their **human capital**—their employees—will realize a competitive advantage. Smarter workers are harder to replicate than software.

To understand today's employee challenges, we must look backwards. In his 1911 book, *Principles of Scientific Management*, Frederick Winslow Taylor laid down the fundamental business principles known as **Taylorism**.

One hundred years ago, as the country was shifting from craft to industrial production, Taylor was highly influential in shaping the birth of the modern American corporation. Many of his ideas are still in use today.

Taylor's biggest and ultimately most destructive idea, drawn from Adam Smith's hypothetical pin factory, was to fragment work into smaller and smaller tasks, so that each worker would do just one portion of a work flow. By creating standard and routine work, skills requirements could be minimized and efficiencies would be gained.

Over time, as organizations grew in size and complexity, this increased specialization required ever-deeper layers of management. Supervisors were needed to link front-line worker tasks, and managers were needed to integrate supervisors' work, and so on. Spans of control, with ratios of one manager to five or six direct reports, became common and micromanagement became prevalent.

Underneath this philosophy lies a set of implicit assumptions about workers that informed this organizational design. Though never stated, Taylor's model was based on the assumption that employees were uneducated, childlike, and solely motivated by money. That's why so much supervision was needed—workers couldn't be trusted to operate on their own.

The result was a paternalistic system where workers worked and managers thought and planned. This separation of responsibilities persists today in industrial-era organizations. Employees lost the essential satisfaction of doing a complete job. Their role devolved into serving as the messy organic parts of assembly lines. Workers also lost their connection to customers, who became an increasingly abstract and distant notion. This model worked well for decades as US companies continued to grow and prosper.

The world has changed, yet vestiges of Taylorism still exist. It's in the design of small jobs requiring repetitive tasks, or the absence of decision-making authority for most workers. It survives in the huge disparity between CEO and frontline worker compensation. According to the Economic Policy Institute, in 1978 the average CEO's pay was 30 times that of the front-line worker. By 1989 it almost doubled to 59x; by 2000 it had ballooned to 383x; and in 2015 it stood at a stunning 523x. At the extreme, Walmart's CEO had a 789x ration, while millions of their employees were assigned 32-hour work weeks so that the company could avoid paying benefits.

Taylorism is alive and well in the hypocritically different ways that organizations deal with workers and managers. As consultant Daniel Markovitz blogged, *"When a plant worker is habitually late and slows down production, they're fired. When an executive is habitually late to meetings, which can cost thousands of dollars of wasted time, nothing happens."* Or, as

Josh Chernin noted, "*Compare the quality of factory worker bathrooms with executive washrooms.*"

Taylorism is embedded deeply into the DNA of most traditional, industrial-era organizations, invisibly woven into the fabric of everyday work. But organizations that began without that heritage approach employee relationships quite differently.

Take Netflix, for example. Examining just one HR policy shows how differently Netflix thinks about employees. The policy is this: Netflix has no vacation policy. That doesn't mean that no one takes time off, it means that there's no set number of days accrued to employees and no policies that grow the number of vacation weeks with tenure. Zero. If someone takes too much vacation time and their work suffers, it's the work that triggers reaction. If too little is taken, that also triggers a concern for an employee's burnout.

Netflix's approach is predicated on its belief that the company hires adults, and adults know how to manage work-life balance. Not everyone fits its culture. There's a several-month tryout period, and if a new hire doesn't fit, they're paid to leave. Netflix only wants employees who accept personal responsibility.

Netflix is an atypical organization. So is Google, which showers its employees with free food, amazing amenities, and widespread stock options. These organizations were born post-Taylorism, which frees them to develop the type of fresh approaches to employee relations which most traditional organizations cannot duplicate.

How can traditional organizations develop smarter workers? Here are six critical moves.

1. INSPIRE THEM WITH A POWERFUL PURPOSE

Travel back in time and imagine that you meet two medieval stonemasons hacking away at rocks. You ask the first, "What are you doing?" and he answers, "I'm chipping some marble."

You ask the second the same question, but he answers, "I'm building a cathedral."

That's the essence and power of purpose. It's much bigger than self-interest. When deployed correctly, a powerful purpose can emotionally connect employees to their organization and leverage that connection to drive high performance. On the other hand, it's really hard to motivate employees about improving shareholder value or to rally the troops on increasing EBITDA.

Nonprofits get it. Participating in an organization that's trying to make the world a better place is motivating. Being part of something bigger than yourself is a powerful inspiration. Consider the mission statement of the New England Center for Children (NECC).

To transform the lives of children with autism worldwide through education, research, and technology

That's a powerful and uplifting statement. When employees arrive at work each day at NECC they see the mission statement at every entry portal. The work they do is difficult, but their mission helps them put those efforts in a bigger, bolder, and more satisfying context. Their tasks are imbued with a higher purpose. If they need to stay late or go an extra mile, they do it in service of their mission.

That's because the results of their work are all around them. They see the children they work with every day. As they walk around their campus they see photos of happy graduates. They receive a stream of data on how their work improves the lives of their students and their families.

Some skeptics might say that NECC is a nonprofit, a mission-driven organization, not focused on maximizing profit and that it needs a meaningful mission because it can't pay as well as for-profit companies.

But compelling missions are not just for charitable organizations. Consider Google's mission: *"To organize the world's information and make it universally accessible and useful."* Or Nike's: *"To bring inspiration and innovation to every athlete in the world (if you have a body you're an athlete)."*

Both statements articulate a higher purpose. Neither mentions money, although both companies are exceptionally profitable. For Google and Nike, profit is the outcome, not the goal in and of itself.

Of course these mission statements are just words: phrases that can be true or hypocritical, clichés or innovative phrases, aspirations or realities. They are also words that can express powerful ideas and shape employee behaviors. Words that can serve as dramatic rallying cries that attract and inspire workers to fulfill their organization's purpose.

When used proactively, organizational mission statements can elevate the collective ambition of the organization far beyond simply making money. Improving shareholder value may have been the dominant business theme over the past 20 years, but it's a dull and counterproductive rallying cry. What rational employee would want to spend unpaid extra hours at work just to help stockholders earn a few extra cents in quarterly earnings?

State Farm's mission, *"To help people manage the risks of everyday life, recover from the unexpected, and realize their dreams,"* is genuinely uplifting. No wonder it has such a high rate of employee retention. Helping members realize their dreams is an emotional reward for employees, which also helps deepen their engagement.

A powerful purpose can also work at process and task levels. A customer service representative can see his or her work as either answering calls or solving customer problems. A software developer can either write lines of code or build a beautiful tool.

A strong mission can serve as a beacon, attracting prospective employees who emotionally connect with that purpose in today's competition for talent. It's not shareholder value that drives our organizations, it's the powerful pull of smart purpose.

2. TURN THEM INTO PROFESSIONALS BY MAKING THEIR JOBS BIGGER

Another approach to making smarter workers is to professionalize them. This is not just a relabeling façade or another HR program. Every existing job can be **automated or augmented**. Depending on the circumstances both can be reasonable options. Doing nothing is not.

The more interesting of the two is augmentation, making jobs bigger and more satisfying. An example of this can be seen at Apple's Genius Bar, where T-shirted technicians fix customer problems for free. Not paid much more than minimum wage, Apple geniuses demonstrate consistent high quality and friendly work delivered with enthusiasm.

Apple chose not to dumb down its retail workers. It could have chosen, as other retailers have, to make employees organic robots and to deconstruct the work into a series of small jobs: receive product, ship product, fix product, return product. Instead, Apple integrated customer service and order fulfillment into a more rewarding job and found ways to motivate their workers. Apple demonstrated that augmenting work turns task workers into **professionals**. But what exactly is a professional?

Imagine you're at a cocktail party, and you meet a stranger and ask him what he does for a living and he replies, "I work for Kaiser." You then meet a second person and ask what she does and she says, "I'm a lawyer."

What a world of difference in these two responses. The first reports a working relationship, the second is a statement of identity. A professional doesn't stop being one when the work day ends, doesn't define their work solely in terms of their employer, and has a distinct pride in their expertise.

That's why "professionalizing" work is better. Here's how one (disguised) company converted task workers into professionals.

Acme, a large equipment manufacturer, was having difficulty with the length of time it was taking to process customer orders. On average, it was taking 23 days from the time a customer verbally agreed to an order with a salesperson to the time a completed contract was delivered for the customer's signature. During those 23 days, the order had to crawl through four Acme departments: order entry, credit checking, terms and conditions, and issuance. Customers were not happy with the long wait. Even more unhappy were Acme's salespeople; every extra minute gave customers an opportunity to change their minds or for a competitor to swoop in.

The sales organization demanded a solution, and a process improvement team was commissioned to fix the problem. The team's ingenious solution was to collapse Acme's paperwork assembly line into a single new job, the Case Manager. The Case Manager's role was to do everything that was needed to get a contract to the customer quickly. Of course, this required significant cross training and new tools. Using an integrated software system, checklists, and templates, the Case Manager could achieve everything that the old process required, but without all the internal handoffs. After 18 months of detailed design and implementation, Acme transitioned to the new way of working. Amazingly, it then only took four hours for orders to be processed.

Why the huge difference? Much of the old way's cycle time was spent waiting between handoffs between the four functional silos. When the four tasks were compressed into a single job, all that time (and the four silos) disappeared.

Acme's story illustrates a recurring pattern of transformation. The company took a complex process composed of simple jobs and transformed it into a simple process filled with complex jobs. The work in the four functional departments was transactional, repetitive, and likely boring for the task workers. On the other hand, the case manager's job is varied and more demanding; they get a line of sight directly to the customer and the satisfaction of doing a complete piece of work.

However, professionalism requires a new set of behaviors. These new traits represent the shift from old-fashioned paternalism to an adult perspective on personal accountability. This means:

- Being held accountable for outcomes for both results and the way they're achieved

- Owning personal responsibility for identifying the skill sets needed to do the work, including knowledge, methods, and tools

- Conducting self-directed problem solving

- Making real-time decision making without frequent escalations upwards

- Working collaboratively within and across work groups with teamwork as the new norm

- Managing your own career

Which would you rather be, a task worker or a professional?

Augmentation requires that you consider, as you redesign your processes, how much decision-making latitude your front-line workers should have. What types of decisions can they make on their own, and when must they ask for managerial permission? How well defined is that line of demarcation, and is it well thought out?

The scope of decision making authority is an extraordinarily important design decision, and it relates to an organization's fundamental view of their performers. Many organizations cling to the old unspoken but pervasive view that front-line workers cannot be trusted with decisions that have financial impact. The consequences that flow from this traditional perspective are littered with safeguards and checks and rechecks far beyond what a rational auditor might require. It doesn't have to be this way; consider these two very different stories:

At a large financial services firm, Customer Service Representatives (CSRs) operate as human tape recorders, documenting customer complaints and then passing them upwards. Their screens provide word-by-word scripts. Improvisation is discouraged and the percentage of calls monitored by managers is high, as is turnover.

At a large chemical company, the CSRs have clear authority to resolve customer complaints and offer settlements up to $x. Anything above $x requires a manager's sign-off. The calls are monitored, but the focus is on training and discovering new internal best practices rather than control. Turnover here is half that of the financial service firm, and customer satisfaction is double.

Which way does your organization think about employees?

None of this will work if employees are not engaged with their jobs. To turn workers into engaged professionals requires the following well known, but infrequently executed actions:

- Provide them with meaningful work that gives them line of sight to outcomes

- Set clear expectations and support them with measured feedback

- Support them with appropriate resources such as tools and training

- Design a supportive work environment that's fair, to enable trust

- Ensure that they have the right information at the right time and place to do their work

- Give them an opportunity to learn and advance

3. INVOLVE EVERYONE IN CHANGE

There have always been two camps in the world of performance improvement, the Changers and the Changees. The Changers have typically been process redesigners, or consultants. Changees are the employees who do the day-to-day work.

In other words, performance improvement has been specialized. Historically, there were precisely defined general roles: workers worked, managers planned, and specialists led change efforts. Perhaps this segmentation was useful in the past, but it is problematic today and probably disastrous for the future. Today's turbulence begets change and more change, and organizations will need more and more performance improvement just to keep up.

Changees often participate in Kaizen events or other improvement workshops, but that's generally a sideline activity, not their primary responsibility.

Given today's competitive pressures, it's imperative to erase these distinctions and marble in performance improvement as a responsibility for every single employee, not just for specialists.

This involvement is more than harnessing the wisdom of the crowd or the expanding power of internal Kickstarters. It's the active cultivation and harvesting of the expertise of the very workers who do the work of the enterprise.

Consider these examples:

- At a consumer products call center, a CSR began using social media on her own initiative, as a way to respond to hard-to-reach customers. This new approach caught on, and customer satisfaction improved.

- A clever ranger at Saguaro National Park suggested that the park implant radio-frequency identification chips in its cactuses to stem the rampant poaching of the plants. Thefts diminished.

- A cross-functional supply-chain team at a chemical company invited an accounts payable representative to sit in with the team to ensure better order coordination. Fewer territorial battles ensued, and lead times shrank.

- A financial manager at a major telecom unilaterally eliminated seven generally unread reports from routine distribution and moved them from scheduled to on-demand delivery. No one noticed.

This revolution in de-specializing change will require significant training investment in a broad set of tools and methodologies. To make this work, employees must be treated as professionals, must care enough about work to want to improve it, and must have the right business knowledge to make positive improvements. Only then will the divide between Changers and Changees end.

4. EDUCATE THEM ABOUT THE BUSINESS

It's amazing how little business knowledge most employees have about their own company or industry. Everyone is so busy catching work thrown to them, doing their tasks, and then throwing the work over to the next worker that the details of upstream or downstream business is invisible to them. The walls of the feudal castle are so high; no one can see over them to understand what's going on in adjacent departments. Work comes, work goes, and what happens afterward is a mystery.

This is exacerbated when cost-management programs slash training and education budgets, resulting in a danger-ous lack of fundamental understanding. Consider the following sad story:

New leadership at a large retailer wanted to assess employ-ees' understanding of the business. The CEO implemented a large-scale survey focused around a single question, "For every dollar that gets rung up at our cash registers, how much profit do we make on that dollar?"

What do you think the average answer was?

The average response from the employees was $.49 on the dollar. This wasn't even close. The retailer, in a good year, made a 3 percent return at best.

Why didn't employees know? You might say that no one told them. Why? Because it wasn't considered part of the job. This was true even though many employees had stock options, and the data was available online.

Yet every single one of those employees makes hundreds of decisions every day, that have a financial impact. Without the right business education, how can they ever make the right decisions?

When HR budgets are slashed and training programs are being cut to the bone, who cares about business education? This same illogic now extends to limiting business travel for training. Do those guilty of these cuts assume that employees know everything they need to know when they walk into the organization on Day One?

By comparison, a major utility developed a two-day business education program that was delivered to every employee. Meter readers, linesmen, and managers all spent time learning how the organization's balance sheet and expense statements were constructed, what customers wanted, how rate cases (price increases) were developed, and how the power industry was evolving. It was an expensive program, but it provided a shared and critical context for every attendee.

Here's the utility's curriculum for creating smarter workers.

Business Understanding

- Who are our customers? Why do they buy from us?

- What are our major customer segments?

- Who are our competitors? What are they good and bad at?

- What are the three biggest trends in our industry?

- How do we make money?

- What are our biggest costs?

- What is our profitability?

Personal

- How does my work impact external customers?

- What are my key metrics?

- What happens before and after me in the flow of work?

- How do I know when I'm doing well?

- How could my work be improved?

By the way, what would be the answer to the same profitability question at your company?

5. LIBERATE EVERYONE FROM OUTMODED POLICIES

Historically, workers had fixed structures. Everyone had precise and detailed job descriptions and reported to a single boss. The job was what you did 100 percent of your time. Your single supervisor was responsible for work oversight, training, and performance feedback. This mechanical model no longer fits today's employee reality. Two issues illustrate this point. Both share a common solution: escape from a fixed to a flexible approach.

Does your day-to-day work match your formal job description? If you're like many, the answer might be: "it once did," "very loosely," "not at all," or "what job description?"

Why does that variance exist?

One culprit may again be organizational anorexia. After years of relentless cost-reduction purges, there's no energy or resources remaining in HR to update formal job descriptions.

Because of competitive pressures, customer demand, and fragmented processes, everyone now wears multiple hats. Whether you're in Accounts Payable, Sales, or Outbound Logistics, the problems of fragmentation are so pervasive and costly that everyone needs to help put Humpty Dumpty back together. Most workers now spend part of their time serving on improvement teams, task forces, or special committee. None of these activities are permanent, so they don't fit the idea of a fixed job description.

Of course all this extracurricular work contributes to meeting mania. Meetings are compensating mechanisms that happen because there's no natural way to connect A to B and B to C, since employees are scattered everywhere into functional silos. So new connective mechanisms are needed.

A final and cynical alternative is that organizations just don't want to know the difference. To formally acknowledge how much and how varied their employees' work is would cause them to adjust pay scales, incentive plans, and structures. Rather than confront all the real dynamism in daily work, many organizations choose denial.

Another archaic limitation is the myth of a single boss. Contemporary reporting relationships are predicated on every employee having just one supervisor. In reality, life is more complicated. To demonstrate the deep complexity of reporting relationships, think about Tom Brady, the New England Patriots quarterback and answer this superficially simple question, *"Who's his boss?"*

- Some would say Bill Belichick, the team's head coach and general manager. He shapes the team and makes all important football decisions.

- Others would say Robert Kraft. He owns the team and signs Brady's paycheck.

- Perhaps it's the team's fans. They are the paying customers, after all.

- Some might suggest the quarterback coach; whose job is to improve Brady's skills.

- Still others say it's the offensive coordinator, who actually calls the plays that Brady executes.

- One could argue that his agent, who negotiates his contracts and secures him promotional deals, is his true boss.

- Finally, a few cynics might say that it's actually Gisele Bündchen, his wife.

None of these answers quite works, does it? The prevailing definition of a "boss" is one who provides supervisory oversight. But oversight is a tiny aspect of what Brady, or any other employee, really needs. Brady receives skills, strategy, coordination, money, and support from a bevy of aligned stakeholders. The question of who's his boss is the wrong question. A better one is: Who helps him succeed? The answer would be more revealing, but much tougher to map out on an organizational chart. It's not so simple, but like Brady, smarter workers need a network of smarter support.

Smart organizations must acknowledge the essential fluidity of work. Organizational agility requires job flexibility. It's time to rethink the fundamental assumptions of roles that have existed for decades. When everything outside the organization is changing rapidly, the inside must adapt as well.

Human Resources must begin this task by rethinking first principles. Before updating job descriptions, HR needs to address their basic purpose: are they for identifying needs for hiring, assigning workers to supervisors, aligning employees with pay bands, clarifying accountabilities, structuring performance evaluations, or all of the above?

That's a heavy burden for any job description, let alone a fluid and malleable one. Perhaps there's no single way to satisfy all of those legitimate needs. Whatever the solution, it's time to acknowledge the gulf between the word and the deed, the paper job description and the reality of workers' day-to-day actions.

In parallel, HR must acknowledge the complexification of traditional reporting relationship and develop new mechanisms to support workers that transcend simple boss-subordinate definition.

One such approach several organizations have used is the Center of Excellence. At one high-tech company, all project managers, independent of specific reporting relationships, participate in the organization's Center of Excellence (CoE) for Project Management. The CoE focuses on:

- Developing and delivering training

- Maintaining a distribution list for content communication and best practice sharing

- Certifying project managers at different levels of expertise

- Aligning project managers to projects based on need and skills

- Conducting long-range capability assessments, looking at the organization's project management needs in the future and developing sourcing strategies to meet those needs

Project managers don't "report" to the CoE, but the CoE plays a critical role in their professional development. This non-hierarchical approach is a perfect example of the complexity in reporting relationships. A CoE is just one example of an innovative mechanism. More are needed.

FREEDOM AND TIME TO THINK

In the first chapter, the epidemic of **busyness** was a major contributor to employees having no time to think. Here are some solutions to the two primary villains of busyness: bad meetings and email mania.

SMART MEETINGS

Why are there so many meetings in the first place?

The first reason is fragmentation; meetings are where peace treaties across feudal boundaries are negotiated. A second reason is that meetings provide a sense of community, a place where everyone knows your name.

Thirdly, it's remarkably easy to call a meeting. As Jim Ware noted, "*In most organizations there are fixed spending limits for expenses at every managerial level, but there are no labor cost limits, so calling a meeting is free to the convener.*" All it takes is access to the calendaring system and poof! Instant meeting. Admins who have no spending authority at all can convene a meeting of senior executives that can cost thousands of dollars. Employees in large organizations have become slaves to their calendars, passively following the demands of their Outlook daily schedule.

Why are there so many bad meetings? What constitutes a bad one? See if this list of dysfunctions feels familiar to you:

- Having no clear purpose for the meeting

- Interruptions from technology beeps distracting and drowning out conversation

- Members arriving late or leaving early

- Using archaic technology for virtual meetings. It's tough enough to deal with latency, lags, and the absence of body language and pheromones, but to use primitive technology makes virtual meetings much harder

- Having no agenda or experiencing the tyranny of the first agenda item (never getting to any other agenda items)

- Avoiding tough topics and difficult decisions

- Providing too many cookies and not enough oxygen

- Developing action items that never get completed

The hours lost and the frustration generated by terrible meetings is enormous. Even more remarkable is that there's a fairly well established set of protocols for having good meetings. They're widely available, mostly common sense, and free.

But because accountability for meetings is diffused (there's no VP of meetings either), there's no executive responsible for this widespread disaster. So bad meetings keep happening, over and over again.

Meetings are necessary. They're where collaboration and information sharing occur. When done well, they provide a sense of community. Instead of the dreadful waste of time and money that most meetings involve, a successful meeting can be a terrifically valuable experience. Smart organizations train all employees on how to have great meetings. Here's a starter set of protocols that should be shared:

1. Start and End on Time: A great method is to calculate the cost of the meeting, post that significant number, and then remind scofflaws of the money they've wasted. Holding short meetings, such as stand-up sessions, also helps. Many organizations have switched to 45-minute meetings to allow transit time between meetings that start on the hour.

2. Operate by Agenda: The best agendas are worked out in advance, and in that agenda every single topic must have:

- a clear duration for the discussion

- a description of the purpose of each item (example: for decision, for discussion)

- some pre-work done in advance

Rigorous discipline is needed to keep the conversation limited to allotted time and to avoid scope creep.

3. Useful Paper on the wall: Really good recurring meetings will have three documents on the wall. The first is a parking lot for good ideas that don't fit the agenda but shouldn't be lost. The second is an action item list. Action items will never be

accomplished unless they have a name and a date attached to them. The third is a list of operating principles the group has agreed on. These commitments might include:

- starting and stopping on time

- doing what you say you'll do

- criticizing ideas, not people

- separating ideation from critique

- standing up for each other's success (no losers on a winning team, etc.)

- responding to team member's emails within a specific period of time

4. Have clear decision rules: The best outcomes happen when there's clarity on how decisions are made and on their surrounding issues. Whether it's the *team leader decides* or *we vote*, clarity is the key. Areas to consider include:

- How will decisions be made? This may be different for different types of issues. For example, the team votes on financial issues but the leader decides on personnel decisions.

- Can decisions be reopened? Many organizations use the principle that decisions cannot be reopened unless compelling new data arises.

- Explicitly announcing when a decision has been reached is important, because sometimes it's not obvious to everyone.

- Can there be publicly dissenting opinions or do Las Vegas rules prevail (what happens in the room, stays in the room)?

What's also needed is a set of organizations policies and rules about meetings. Meeting mania should not be allowed to continue to waste enormous amounts of time. It's not just bad meetings that are so expensive. Many meetings never should be held in the first place.

These rules should include protocols on:

- Who can convene a meeting, and whose approval may be needed to book one?

- How to cost out a meeting, and who pays for that?

- How long should meetings be (the shorter the better)?

- What alternatives are available, and what criteria to use for each need for collaboration?

- How to track action items for accountability purposes?

To make all of these suggestions workable, ongoing training on meeting hygiene is needed. In addition, holding people accountable for bad or unneeded meetings would also help minimize the pain.

SMART EMAIL

There are three theaters of action that can defeat email mania:

1. Personal Actions

   - Become a Zero In-Box success, by using email folders as personal file cabinets.

   - Send less, get less.

   - Filter for a single recipient. Most systems allow prioritization by such attributes.

   - Unsubscribe rigorously.

- Use subject lines for responses.

- Experiment with longer no-email periods to begin training correspondents about response times.

- Post communication-off messages for evenings, weekends, and vacations.

2. Institutional Policies that need power or policy

  - Assign clear executive accountability for email management.

  - Monitor, then measure employee time on email to calculate its hidden enterprise costs. Use this to build case for action, change, and accountability.

  - Disable "reply all" option; that means senders would have to type in all the names of recipients, slowing down massive email chains driven by CYA.

  - Make emails disappear. One organization evaporates all email after 90 days of first sending.

  - Set up an Intranet dedicated to data requests.

  - Limit distribution lists to 10 or fewer.

  - Develop clear and strict policies for hours of sending and response to limit evening and weekend usage.

  - Develop experiments for digital detox times.

  - Some countries are taking the lead in taming email. France has outlawed email after work hours for companies with more than 50 employees.

  - The issues of bad meetings and email mania are enormous and pervasive. Because they're new and don't fit traditional business models, no one owns them, no one measures them, and no one improves them. The costs in terms of lost time is uncounted but vast. To do nothing about the time wasted on email and bad meetings is really stupid. Smart organizations fix these problems.

SMARTER WORKERS SOLUTION SUMMARY

- Communicate a powerful purpose at all levels to enhance employee engagement. Make work more than a job.

- Professionalize jobs through either automation or augmentation. There's no middle ground anymore.

- Educate all employees on your business basics. Every employee makes decisions every day that have financial consequences; make sure they have the right context.

- Fix email mania and meeting madness by acknowledging the problem and developing enterprise solutions. Assign accountability for these orphan productivity problems.

Chapter 8
SMART BEHAVIORS: FROM WORDS TO ACTIONS

> *"Culture eats strategy for breakfast"*
> — attributed to Peter Drucker

Leadership's most important role may be to shape the organization's culture by articulating a set of shared values. But culture manifests in the actual **behaviors** of employees. It is in the realm of action that what we say becomes who we are. In other words, values are an attempt to modify culture, but that success can only be assessed though behaviors.

Ideally, there would be perfect harmony between words and deeds, aspirations and actions, values and behaviors. But frequently, behaviors conflict with stated values. When that happens, it's only action that can be managed and measured.

All organizations must start with honesty and integrity as baseline behaviors, but these are just table stakes. What's needed are new behaviors that precisely fit the requirements of our era.

To be useful, the following seven smart behaviors must be marbled into the fabric of the organization. To be real, they must show up in hiring, performance evaluation, and promotion. To be communicated, they must be modeled by executives and demanded of employees. These behaviors can't simply be aspirational; they must be performed widely. As Richard Pascale, author of *Managing on the Edge*, once wisely noted, *"It's easier to act your way into a new way of thinking, than to think your way into new ways of acting."*

These behaviors can't just exist at the organizational level. They must also be embodied in employees. That means **you**. Answer the following questions for both your organization and yourself.

1. COMPLETELY CUSTOMER-CENTRIC

How customer-centric is your organization?

- _ We say we are, but our actions prove we aren't.
- _ We say we are, and our actions back that up.
- _ We'd like to be but are not.
- _ We don't have customers, only victims.

The Golden Rule is true: those who have the gold make the rules. As competition intensifies, power inevitably flows down-stream, and customers are the beneficiaries. No matter what you call them—consumers, clients, patients, or guests—if these customers aren't happy, they'll leave you. Underserve them at your peril, unless you're an airline.

No one says they hate their customers. But some act that way. American Airline's mission statement says that they want flying to be friendly and special. Was your luggage charge friendly, and did you find that tiny seat special? Were you able to easily cash in your frequent flyer miles? Airline companies routinely treat their best customers worst. How long until that comes back to bite them? Will it ever?

What does customer-centricity look like?

- Every employee understands their organization's customer value proposition.

- Every employee knows who customers are, and why they buy from their organization.

- Incentives up and down and across the organization are

equitably balanced between shareholders, customers, and employees.

If the most dangerous place at your organization is standing in front of the elevators at 5 p.m., you're not a customer-centric organization. If a visitor can't tell what business you're in from seeing your visitor's lobby, you're not a customer-centric business either. Enter Valvoline's headquarters in Lexington, Kentucky, and there's a race car in the lobby; enter Fidelity's lobby in Boston, and there are pictures of customers and their children adorning every wall with letters thanking Fidelity for its financial stewardship.

Here's what customer-centricity really looks like. Recently, a customer entered an REI store in the middle of a rain storm. He was soaking wet because his raincoat had split at the seam. When he explained his predicament to a salesperson and asked where the raincoat section was, she suggested that instead of buying a new $200 high-tech jacket, he purchase a $20 can of waterproofing spray that would immediately repair his coat. That's what he did, and that's customer centricity.

2. AMBITIOUS YET HUMBLE

Your organization

- _ Is playing to win
- _ Is playing not to lose
- _ Is playing at playing
- _ Is winning, but still not satisfied

Look closely at any image of a Roman general being celebrated for a major victory, and you'll see another rider in his chariot. That second person, a slave, is whispering into the general's ear. His words echo from Rome to every winning organization today, *"All glory is fleeting; this too shall pass."*

Winners rarely consider themselves winners and are seldom self-congratulatory. Things change, and today's victor can easily be tomorrow's victim. A relentless focus on improvement is needed to sustain success.

A public statement released by American Express's leadership team expresses both ambition and humility: *"We want to be the company that puts us out of business."*

Ambitious organizations have an unrelenting dissatisfaction with the status quo. Amazon demonstrated this by releasing the Kindle, a direct competitor to printed books, its primary product. Amazon disrupted itself.

When change is accelerating, there's no time to stop and admire past success. Organizations that have adapted to nonstop change never take their successes too seriously. As Al Jolson once said after receiving 30 minutes of thunderous applause at a major concert, *"You ain't seen nothing yet."*

3. DOUBLY ACCOUNTABLE

What happens at your organization when managers don't meet their commitments?

- _   Nothing at all
- _   A string of stern warnings
- _   Reassignment or outplacement
- _   Promotion

Few actions cause more employee cynicism than failing to hold executives accountable for their commitments. A commitment is a contract: If you provide the resources, I'll achieve an important outcome. When senior managers fail to deliver the promised results and nothing happens, the value of internal contracts is degraded. Because organizations have few secrets, the problem is obvious and trust is broken. In times of intense competition, making and keeping commitments is the key to sustained success.

There's a second critical dimension to accountability. What matters is not just fulfilling your commitments, but also the way that you fulfill them.

As an unnamed Fortune 10 company learned, a culture of success worship had created a host of serious ethical and behavioral problems. Many high performers were leaving the company due to the misbehavior of colleagues. To remedy this culturally driven problem, the company's management created the following simple matrix (Exhibit 8) to clearly and explicitly identify what outcomes and what approaches were needed in the organization's future. This matrix now serves as the foundation for all employee performance evaluations.

Accountability Matrix

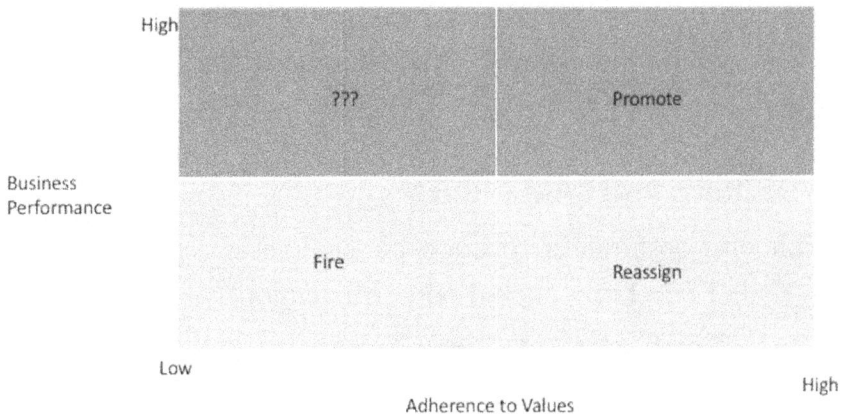

Business Performance (vertical axis: High to Low), Adherence to Values (horizontal axis: Low to High). Top left: ???; Top right: Promote; Bottom left: Fire; Bottom right: Reassign.

The top right cell is easy. High performance achieved the right way became the path to promotion. In the lower left, poor performance and poor behavior leads to the exit door. The lower right is a bit more complex. The combination of poor business performance with high adherence to value often means that there was a bad fit between an employee and a job, and reassignment might be the best next step.

The upper left cell, where high business performance meets low adherence to values, is the most revealing of all. It's a window into the soul of an organization. What happens to unscrupulous high performers? Are they excused? Do results only matter? At the large company, these high-performing miscreants were often promoted and lavished rewarded, making a mockery of aspirational values. To dramatically change the culture, a number of obvious members of this quadrant were publicly fired. Their old bad behaviors needed a new organizational behavior to begin turning back the cynicism of the past.

Sadly, it's not uncommon that business success trumps bad behavior. When there are exceptions, everyone knows that it's just the bottom line that matters. Do those organizations that say that they value integrity but reward bad behavior think their employees are stupid or blind? Don't leaders realize how revealing these decisions are? It's only when the choices are tough, that an organization sees what's real and what's just words.

How accountable are your high performers?

4. DECISIVE AND DATA DRIVEN

What wins arguments in your organization?

- _ HIPPO (highest paid person's opinion)
- _ Passion
- _ Data
- _ Exhaustion
- _ Incriminating photos

How frustrating it must be to work in a consensus culture. At a large multinational equipment company, an endless debate on the issue of centralization paralyzed the organization for five years as leadership waited for a clear consensus to emerge. Getting along was prized higher than getting it right, so polite conversation went on forever and produced no resolution. This inaction cost the company millions of dollars of profit as faster-moving competitors took customers away. At a second company, the public smiles of collegial consensuality hid a vicious behind-closed-doors set of cut-throat behaviors. Consensus was a cover for Machiavellian deceit.

At a third large business, a valued behavior is processing information quickly and making decisions without perfect knowledge. Leadership realized that there was never going to be a moment of perfect data and absolute certainty, so managers and employees across the company were given wide latitude to make decisions quickly, when needed.

In fast-moving times, decisiveness is critical. When you're in a race car speeding at 150 miles an hour, and a competitor tries to pass you, you can't spend minutes pondering your response—you have to act, and act quickly. Thirty years ago, when change was sluggish and evolutionary, there was time to slowly contemplate options. When time is measured in nanoseconds, crisp decision-making is required.

Both analysis paralysis and the glacial development of consensus are deadly behaviors in turbulent times. Victory will always go to the swift and decisive.

Throughout history, intuition and experience have dominated decision making and served organizations well. Although they are still important, we now live in the age of data-driven decision making.

What does this look like? At the leading edge, unsurprisingly, are professional service firms, where analysis is king. One major consulting company's mantra, *"Show me the data,"* is repeated over and over every day, illustrating the value that information has for them. Every tool the firm uses is a way to get, interpret, or use data. Hunches must be supported by data; guesses are for amateurs.

Data-driven organizations take measurement seriously, because data tells the truth. It is an objective mirror of reality, showing what is, not what we'd like.

For these organizations, analytics become a new common language. Measurement is not just a tool, it's a new way of managing the business. If bad news is hidden, and incentives trump truth, or if HIPPO reigns, then measurement will only be a game, not a smart tool.

You can see data-driven behaviors in the number and depth of feedback mechanisms, in the size of the budget spent on analytic training, and in the elevation of master data management. These organizations treat the search and creation of a single source of truth for all key data elements as a strategic objective.

Data-driven organizations give employees time to think, and the most successful ones provide unstructured time. 3M gives all employees one afternoon a week for tinkering, learning, and thinking. This has consistently facilitated the achievement of their annual goal of 30 percent of revenue derived from new products. It's not just innovation but reflection that drives their success.

5. COLLABORATIVE TOGETHER

Is teamwork really valued at your organization?

- It's lip service. We say that we want it, but don't reward it.
- Power is a zero-sum game here. I can only win if you lose.
- Collaboration is embedded in all our management systems.
- Can I get some help answering that question?

No one has all the answers. In today's complex environment, it takes a diverse set of perspectives and capabilities to generate a steady stream of solutions. It really does take everyone working together to solve the challenges of sustained organizational success. As Abraham Lincoln proclaimed, *"A house divided against itself cannot stand."*

Think about the use of pronouns in your organization. When "we" replaces "me" and "you" becomes "us," the benefits of teamwork will appear.

Collaboration is not a synonym for group hugs. You don't see placid serenity at truly collaborative organizations, you see vigorous debate. Great organizations escape the tyranny of group think by fostering contention and argumentation. The smartest ideas are forged in the crucible of intense discussion. That only happens when there's trust that stems from collaboration. Then it's safe to debate. The disagreement isn't personal, it's a collaborative search for the best answers.

A large nonprofit uses the phrase *"tension is healthy, conflict is not,"* as a way to calibrate collaboration. The organization relishes and supports its resident contrarians.

Collaboration is visible in shared metrics and incentives. When it's working, it lives in cosponsored programs and is supported by clear decision rules and well-defined roles. It's transparent. At IBM, all calendars are visible to everyone. The specifics are blanked out but availabilities are clearly marked.

Without collaboration, politics and territoriality dominate behaviors. Both are unpleasant and dysfunctional. When organizations say they value teamwork, but leaders put themselves first all the time, do they think employees are stupid or blind?

6. INTELLECTUALLY CURIOUS

How would you describe your organization's risk profile?

    _   We hate risk. All risk is bad risk.
    _   We're risk averse. We've been burned before so we

actively limit risk taking.

– Risks "R" us. We're adrenaline junkies.

– We accept some risk but hedge through careful experimentation.

Smart organizations treat thinking and learning as real work, not as extracurricular options. Others, although they may not admit it, suffer from the stultification brought about by ancestor worship. The memories of their golden eras linger far beyond their glory days. A scary quote attributed to Kafka describes this syndrome: *"When memories exceed dreams, the end is near."*

Driving into the future while looking through the rear-view mirror creates an aversion to risk. *"We're a giant status quo machine that kills innovation quickly and easily,"* one senior manager confided. The mantra at similar organizations could be, *"If it isn't broken, don't fix it."* But when it does break, it's too late to fix it.

The path to real organizational learning runs through structured experiments. It's easy to be fooled in a conference room when teams inhale one another's exhaust.

The real world is far more complex than can be imagined in a conference room full of words and paper. It takes testing to develop a dramatic new process design or create an innovative new service. That's how you achieve the intended outcome.

Experimentation requires making mistakes, and the key to success is making those inevitable mistakes early and inexpensively. As the Toyota Production System says, "Cherish your mistakes." That's how learning happens, but for organizations that punish failure, mistakes are avoided at all costs, which dooms learning and innovation.

Common behaviors in intellectually curious organizations include:

- Aggressively questioning assumptions combined with a nonstop searching for answers.

- A high level of comfort with ambiguity and living in the open question.

- Willingness to declare a breakdown, and fearlessly confronting problems rather than resorting to denial, delusion, or witch-hunts.

In some cultures, creating intellectual curiosity is difficult because challenging the status quo is seen as disrespectful. Here's how one organization addressed this limitation.

At Gamesa, the largest cookie and cracker company in Mexico (now owned by PepsiCo), behavior change was the hardest aspect of its transformation from a functional to a process-based organization. Jose Luis Prado, the CEO, personally led this multiyear program designed to dramatically improve the company's productivity and profitability. After several years, Gamesa had reengineered many of its processes but still had not generated the expected results.

Prado believed that Gamesa's problem was in trying to operate new process designs but with old behaviors. In particular, it was having trouble encouraging employee innovation. In the past, employees never challenged their managers. They thought it would be disrespectful to offer innovative solutions. The implicit operating model had been that the workers' role was to quietly work and the manager's job was to think. If this reticence to suggest changes continued, success would be in jeopardy. Gamesa's front-line workers really did know where the problems were and what the solutions might be. But getting them to share those insights was the challenge.

Prado knew that Gamesa would never be successful if that old behavior continued. How could he get his employees to respectfully challenge authority and become comfortable suggesting improvements?

He and his senior team developed a plan to publicly model the behaviors they wanted employees to emulate. Leadership proceeded to script a public debate in which several of the executives would challenge Prado's ideas. Instead of getting angry at this disrespect, Prado would actively listen and then agree with their arguments, demonstrating that challenging a senior person's ideas was safe and acceptable. The senior team repeated this drama a number of times across the organization over the next few weeks, and eventually, behaviors began to change. Of course, there was no immediate transition, but a visible shift had occurred.

FINAL EXAM

There are a number of problematic phrases common to troubled organizations. How many of these acronyms can you identify?

    a. NIH

    b. IDWIT

    c. INMJ

    d. TTWWADI

    e. IDMB

    f. BISS

(Answers in box at right)

a. NIH: Not Invented Here
b. IDWIT: I Do What I'm Told
c. INMJ: It's Not My Job
d. TTWWADI: That's The Way We've Always Done It
e. IDMB: I Did My Best
f. BISS: Because I say so

CHAPTER NINE:
SMART ENTERPRISE: FROM FEUDALISM TO FEDERALISM

"Things fall all apart; the center cannot hold;
Mere anarchy is loosed upon the world"
W.B. YEATS, THE SECOND COMING

Now we come to the enterprise, addressing the entire organization as one singular unit. Smart enterprises find ways to optimize all organizational resources with a goal of synergy. Synergy occurs when the sum of the whole is greater than its parts. It can only be achieved when organizations focus all of their energy and resources on external success, instead of wasting them on internal strife.

Synergy is the only way traditional organizations can win.

When large organizations effectively harness their resources, they can beat disruptive competitors. When they operate as one integrated entity, they are unstoppable. But when they behave as a group of loosely independent fiefdoms, their scale advantage turns against them. Fragmentation only leads to doom in today's turbulence.

An acronym for today's competitive environment is VUCA— Volatile, Uncertain, Complex, and Ambiguous. As one business unit leader bemoaned, *"These are treacherous times. The past is no longer a guide into our future, and the market is changing faster than we are. As that differential grows, so do our risks."* Compounding the complexity of this environment is the technology typhoon.

At a societal level, this turbulence is causing widespread decentralization and polarization. A loss of trust in major institutions has occurred, and cohesion at all levels suffers. Confusion reigns. When you've lost your bearings, it's only natural to hunker down and focus on the local and the familiar.

Organizationally, these trends weaken the center as power flows from corporate headquarters out to the periphery. When business units and functional and geographic leaders power up, the strength of the corporate core declines, leading to:

- Difficulty establishing standards. While many organizations attempt to create consistency, few succeed in overcoming resistance and active noncompliance. It's easy to articulate standards but much tougher to enforce them. Noncompliance leads to multiple standards, an expensive oxymoron.

- Limited processes sharing or commonality, as business units and geographies take control and customize work to suit local needs. Fewer internal best practices are adopted. This same dynamic occurs on the product side as local units battle around common pricing, promotions, programs, packaging, etc. While business units can benefit from this tailoring, aggregate costs often dwarf local benefits. Still, the local prevails.

- Redundancy everywhere as hundreds of disconnected improvement projects and multiple prioritization pools clog up the improvement pipeline. Multiple ERPs and databases create unneeded costs.

- Growing variation in HR policies as the number of profit centers increase and incentives localize, making it harder to move employees around the organization.

- Weakened traditional adjudication methods, such as

enterprise committees and task forces, which used to serve as alignment mechanisms.

THE FUTILITY OF FEUDALISM

All these symptoms of fragmentation are caused by feudalism. In medieval feudalism, there was no concept of a unified country. The model was based on a weak king who ruled by allocating power and turf to strong nobles who then ruled their local territories. Allegiance in these fiefdoms was to the local nobleman first, and the king second. The independence of the fiefdoms counterbalanced the power of the center. In feudalism, the ties that connect the parts to the whole are weak, making for weak kingdoms. When fragmentation is the norm, synergy is minimal.

Synergy occurs when an organization presents a single face to the outside world, when best practices are swiftly shared and adopted, when there's a single source of data truth, and when internal transaction costs are minimized.

The motto for fragmented enterprises can be borrowed from the cartoonist Walt Kelly, whose major character, Pogo, once declared, *"We have met the enemy and he is us."*

Rebalancing power is difficult. Power is zero sum, to give it requires taking it. Traditional mechanisms such as task forces or executive committees are often used for this purpose. But these temporary tools are insufficient to solve the deep underlying problem of power imbalance.

In the past, the most common solution for reallocating power was structural reorganization. Most organizations have redrawn the lines and boxes of their organizational charts hoping that a new structure would solve all their problems. Few received any benefit.

That's because structure is a weak lever for real change.

Organizational charts only show power and money, not the actual work of the organization. Changing reporting relationships rarely improves business performance. It always causes confusion and months of adjustment. Creating new profit centers is an accounting mechanism, not a transformational action. Recalculating transfer prices is a total waste of time.

Besides, any organizational chart is inherently inaccurate. No large enterprise ever has just one organizational structure; it will have many, all operating simultaneously. Organizations are complex entities with multiple simultaneous axes including geographies, functions, business units, product groups, market segments, and end-to-end processes. Each is orthogonal, i.e. perpendicular to each other in non-Euclidean dimensions.

No chart can ever capture this complexity, as each axis represents a specific perspective and tries to optimize it. No matter how a chart may be drawn, the goals of these axes are always in tension, and the organizational chart cannot resolve it.

Restructuring is a failed attempt to impose clarity on an increasingly complex world. Another approach is required to strengthen the core.

FEDERALISM IS NEEDED

"No one is smarter than everyone"

—Attributed to many

Puny or superficial change cannot reverse the flow of power away from the center. A dramatically different operating model, which inculcates a better sharing of power, needs to be instituted.

An operating model is the framework that allows an organization to achieve its mission. It's a superstructure that sits above structure that aligns all organizational elements toward a common goal.

There are several fundamentally different basic operating models, each containing different balances of power and authority. On one end of the spectrum are conglomerates, where independent units are loosely tied together for financial reporting purposes. No synergy is sought or delivered, and the center is very weak. Power is concentrated in the units.

At the other extreme are tightly integrated global entities. These can be easily identified by the frequent use of the number 1, as in a single instance of an ERP, one enterprise strategy, one face to the customers, one of everything. This singular unity is achieved by an all-powerful center that ensures consistency and commonality.

Federalism sits between the two. Marked by clear delineations of power and decision rights between the center and the parts, it represents the best of both worlds. Although many actions are left to business units or geographies, there are also non-negotiable requirements, such as participation in shared services and common data definitions. Federalism produces a strong balance of power and equilibrium across an organization. With the right design, federalism is the way to achieve both economies of scale and appropriate local customization.

Look at Singapore. Despite size limitations, it has achieved remarkable success in trade, health, and high technology. Singapore's federalism is embedded in its autocratic democracy. The ruling party drives synergy along clear rules, giving the country a clear balance between government power and individual rights.

To understand this, consider the solar system. The planets circle the sun in stable orbits due to the balance of two opposing forces: centrifugal force, which pushes the planets away from the sun, and centripetal force, which pulls the planets in toward the sun. If one is too strong, the planets fly out into space, if the other dominates, planets crash into the sun.

Together they produce equilibrium, our 365-day year.

To continue this metaphor, in many traditional organizations, the centrifugal force has overwhelmed the centripetal, as parts of the organization have distanced themselves from the center. As the following story illustrates, federalism is the best response to this growing imbalance.

FROM CONGLOMERATE TO FEDERALIST

A large manufacturer facing pricing pressure in three of its four independent business units decided to redesign its operating model. Historically, the organization had been a traditional conglomerate with each business operating independently. The businesses were vertically integrated, each having its own HR, IT, Finance, and Legal departments.

The duplication was costly, so the first move was to combine those four functions into a shared service center. After a year, costs had diminished by 33 percent and service levels were higher. The biggest benefits were derived from shrinking the huge number of legacy IT systems. Cutting the maintenance of those eliminated systems alone justified the entire change.

Rather than declaring victory, the company then made a more radical operating model change: It pulled the entire supply chain out of each of the four businesses and created a new enterprise logistics group, which cut the size of each unit in half.

The goal was twofold. First, to gain major cost savings through synergies and economies of scale. Over the first two years, the change produced enormous benefits as the company consolidated warehouses and eliminated many logistical redundancies.

The second goal was to shift business unit leadership's focus inside out. Instead of spending time with suppliers and worrying about shipping rates, the CEO wanted business leaders spending more time with customers and thinking about their unmet needs and innovative pricing strategies.

As the business moved from conglomerate to federalist, costs shrank and synergies grew. The most critical enabler of this transformation was the redesign of the company's governing processes. For example, in the past, the company had four independent strategies, each developed in different ways. At the end, they had one enterprise Strategic Planning process that drove their transformation. By looking at the entire enterprise, new internal and external opportunities were identified and executed. Their Strategic Planning processes became the glue that fused the new organization together.

GOVERNING PROCESSES

A process is a set of tasks that creates an outcome of value. This definition is true at end-to-end enterprise processes or for small workflows. No matter what type of organization, there are essentially three categories of processes.

The first type of process is core or value-added processes. These basic building blocks include new product development, order fulfillment, and customer acquisition. Core processes are the heart of any organization. They create value for customers, and they're the reason the organization exists. Core processes generate the revenue that funds the enterprise. High-performing core processes are the primary execution engine that delivers short-term-success.

The second category, enabling processes, only exist to support core processes and provide no direct customer value. They consume rather than create resources. Examples include processes that support Human Resources, IT, Legal, and Finance. Though necessary, they are rarely the source of competitive advantage.

The third category, governing processes, serves as the essential mechanism for ensuring successful federalism. The role of governing processes, which align and coordinate all other processes, is to operate across the organization to create synergy.

The most important governing process, strategic planning, informs all other processes on which goals and actions are, well, most strategic. It's the steering wheel for the smart enterprise.

Other governing processes include capability management, risk mitigation, master data management, and strategic execution.

While core processes create short-term success, it's governing processes, which operate with longer time horizons, that are responsible for sustained success.

Weak governing processes cause feudalism. Core processes are similar to human ego and id, demanding short-term satisfaction. Governing processes serve as the superego, keeping short-term urges from overwhelming long-term needs.

It's the job of governing processes to ensure organizational cohesion, to optimize assets, and to create lasting value for all key stakeholders. While short-term competitive advantage comes from better core processes, long-term advantage can only be generated by strong governing processes.

STRATEGIC PLANNING AND THE THREE GREAT TENSIONS

Zillions of books have been written about strategic planning. This is not one of them. Without question, strategic planning is *primus inter pares*, the single most important process for any organization. Without a well-designed and well-executed strategic planning process, winning is impossible; it is how resources and assets are deployed to achieve the organization's most important goals.

Technically, strategic planning is an abbreviated name for the entire process of Policy Deployment (Hoshin Kanri). Its pyramid descends from the top—the mission—down to the details of strategy execution. By definition, Policy Deployment is the way to ensure that all parts of the organization aim at the same target.

The most important components of Policy Deployment are:

- Purpose: Mission, Vision, and Values

- Strategic Principles

- Long-Term Strategy

- Annual Strategy

- Key Metrics, Actions, and Programs

- Operating Plans

- Linked goals and actions from the top to the bottom of the organization

Within this enormous sweep, the **Three Great Tensions** must be resolved to achieve the synergies of federalism.

First, the mission statement must address the critical issue of *"Who do we serve and in which order?"* It's easy to list the usual suspects (shareholders, customers, employees), but it's much more difficult to prioritize them. They can't all be first. The needed output should be a clear statement of stakeholder precedence and rationale.

Second, strategic principles must clarify the power of the center and the parts (the business version of state and federal rights). Just a few principles can serve as the foundation for resolving many detailed issues. Without clear resolutions, civil wars are inevitable. These principles serve as the enterprise's constitution.

Finally, the long-term strategy needs to clarify the proportions of total resource investment between today and tomorrow
and between small change and big change. What's needed is
a model that clarifies the nature of future investments versus
short-term needs.

There's no right or wrong way to resolve these tensions.
Solutions can be vastly different depending on the organization's basic operating design or strategy. When there's no
resolution, there's cognitive dissonance and the absence of
organizational alignment. When there's no alignment, there's
chaos. When there's chaos, everyone loses.

WHO DO YOU SERVE?

It's simplistic to assume that organizations only serve customers. An enterprise cannot exist without customers, but there
are other key stakeholders who also have needs that must be
satisfied. Employees, regulators, suppliers, shareholders, and
communities matter.

Still, it's not possible to serve them all equally. There are
tradeoffs inherent in every business decision, from service to
cost, from cost to pollution, from pollution to wages, and from
wages to dividends. Prioritization is needed. Some organizations never address the issue at all, leading to confusion.

Richard Branson, leader of The Virgin Group, states his
stakeholder precedence clearly, "Put the staff first, customers
second, and shareholders third."

Smart organizations use more than words to demonstrate
their priorities. The Four Season hotel chain has several
unusual practices. For example, before it renovates a hotel, it
upgrades employee facilities.

Johnson & Johnson's Credo, a mission document that's lasted
more than 100 years, is structured around J&J's key stakeholders.

The Credo puts doctors, nurses, and patients first and foremost, followed by suppliers, employees, and the communities in which J&J operates. Last comes stockholders. The Credo makes the logic of this sequence very clear:

> *"Our final responsibility is to our stockholders. Business must make a sound profit. We must experiment with new ideas. Research must be carried on, innovative programs developed and mistakes paid for. New equipment must be purchased, new facilities provided and new products launched. Reserves must be created to provide for adverse times. When we operate according to these principles, the stockholders should realize a fair return."*

Even in the same industry, there are rational organizations that choose different stakeholder priorities. It's evident that Wal-Mart serves customers as the means to profitability, while Costco's logic is happy employees make happy customers. The huge differential in employee compensation dramatically makes this point. In 2015, the average hourly pay for Costco was $20.89 versus $12.81 for Walmart.

STRATEGIC PRINCIPLES

Strategic Principles define the rules of the road, the ways that power is distributed across the enterprise. This common foundation helps resolve detailed issues consistently. For some organizations, high-level statements are nothing but pure apple pie and motherhood. They're useless for resolving complex problems because they're just trite truisms, like "We focus on value-added for our customers."

Smart enterprises take a different approach. Their principles have an edge, which comes from clearly expressing a position. An edgy principle is one that rational people may disagree upon.

It's one that can be thoughtfully argued from both sides. "Honesty is a good policy" isn't edgy; who can disagree with that? On the other hand, "We will conduct maximum compliance with all environmental regulation" could be argued both ways. Edge makes principles useful. Defining organizational power requires sharp clarity, as these useful principles demonstrate:

- "We optimize for the enterprise first, business units second." One implication would be that if a poor performing unit needed to borrow staff from a high-performing unit, that would be acceptable if the change benefited the enterprise even if it harmed the lending unit.

- "Business leaders are responsible for the outcomes of both the resources they control and those they share." Many managers whine that they can only be held accountable for resources they control completely, that they can't be held responsible for their colleague's incompetence. This principle is designed to foster collaboration by aligning compensation with teamwork.

- "Data and data definitions are owned by the enterprise." Data is an asset whose value diminishes with contradiction.

- "No business unit 'owns' staff." Employees are resources to be deployed for enterprise value creation.

- "The more internal the process the more standard it must be." This paves the way for shared services and standards.

One specialty chemical company used a pair of Strategic Principles to directly shape its investments. During strategic planning, it sorted the organization's processes into three buckets: Critical—those processes that provided competitive

advantage; Important—processes that made a market difference; and Necessary—those processes where statutory
compliance was the only goal. The first principle required it
to grade its processes on the curve, ensuring that only 20
percent of processes could be deemed Critical, 60 percent
Important, and 20 percent Necessary. The second strategic
principle was that critical processes would receive 80 percent
of the improvement budget while important processes would
share 20 percent. There would be no investment in the third
category.

To be effective, these Strategic Principles must be explicit
and precise, with no shades of gray. When enforced, the value
of these principles shows up in many ways, facilitating compliance to standards, clarifying accountability for resources, and
most important, clearly defining the relationship between the
enterprise and the parts.

TODAY VS. TOMORROW

The tension between Today vs. Tomorrow resides everywhere.
In business we ask, "Do we spend to improve this quarter's
performance or defer gratification by investing in tomorrow's
capabilities?" In politics, we fight over immediate tax cuts or
infrastructure investments that will only pay off years into the
future. In personal finances, we ping-pong between the seduc-
tion of buying more cool stuff versus putting aside money for
retirement savings.

In the business world, the winner of this tension is obvious.
Today is the victor, hands down. When short-term financial
results are the measure of success, longer-term investment is
subordinated.

Once again, the urgent beats out the important.

There's little transparency in this area. Few organizations

explicitly measure their resource allocation this way. But viewing how organizations spend their scare resources like money and executive attention can be very revealing.

Several years ago, my colleague Brad Power and I developed a simple model that outlined four major domains of future investment as a way to target and track them. Our idea was to connect the dots across product development, human resource, and improvement silos to derive an enterprise perspective on the balance between today and tomorrow spending and big and little change. Often, these issues are addressed in the details; we wanted to elevate those details into a bigger picture. To do this, we identified four broad investment options.

1. Today's Work. The Execution Engine is voracious and the whirlwind of today's work can consume everybody's attention and all resources if unchecked.

2. Incremental Improvement. This is the sum of the investment in operational excellence and Continuous Improvement. It's rooted in medium-term benefits.

3. Incremental Innovation. This represents medium-term improvements in products, services, and capabilities.

4. Discontinuous Change. This category represents any major step-function change such as major reengineering, acquisition, new product categories, etc.

5. This model should be used both for diagnosis and prescription. It can be used to estimate the current proportions and define the target spending. It can also widen the discourse on the best ways to allocate scarce resources.

6. Obviously, no organization can ignore either the needs of today or its long-term requirements. It's never either

or. The key is finding the optimal balance between these competing opposites. Rather than reactively discovering its proportions, smart enterprises should target their allocation across these categories. That's why smart organizations need a disciplined approach to allocating their finite resources around the future.

STRATEGIC EXECUTION

Only a smart enterprise can cure Project-itis. Here's how one company did it.

A Fortune 100 company began experiencing trouble staffing major improvement projects. Sponsors across the organization were having increased difficulty finding available employees to join their teams. The executive committee was mystified by this pervasive problem.

The CEO took this issue on himself. After a few weeks of investigation, he discovered that nobody knew how many projects were active across the company. Managers knew about their individual projects, of course, but no one could tell him the organizational total. Even worse, no one had any idea what their project success rate was.

So the CEO asked one of his senior managers, Ken, to investigate. Ken's first move was to conduct a thorough inventory of all the projects underway in the company.

It took a month of detective work, but Ken came back with an astounding number. There were more than 1,400 active projects in the inventory. There were big ones, small ones, red ones, secret ones, where the initiator didn't want his project to be seen, as well as redundant and conflicting projects.

It became clear that immediate action was needed. Leadership convened a task force, led again by Ken (yet another project, as they ironically noted) to gather information on the benefits, costs, time frames, membership, and status of every project, none of which was easily available or accessible. The team estimated that in the past 3 years, the company's success rate had been around 10 percent.

Once Ken shared the project data, leadership began a rigorous prioritization process. Their initial goal was to slash the project portfolio in half. Although each project had been launched with positive intent, the total number of efforts was unsustainable. So 700 projects were terminated and their teams disbanded.

With fewer projects to review, the portfolio was reprioritized and cut in half again. Both times the criteria were based on ROI and implementation difficulty. After the second round, roughly 300 projects remained.

The impact of this triage was immediate and valuable, with surviving projects upgrading membership quality and quantity and better project managers aligning with more strategic projects.

Most important, the 300 represented a project portfolio balanced by beneficiary—customer, shareholder, employee, short- and long-term timeframes, level of risk, and area of the business. The company could only create this optimized portfolio by surveying all the projects.

The company developed a project process, several related Strategic Principles, and a Project Management Office (PMO). One of the principles stated that no one could unilaterally launch a project, that all candidate projects needed to fill out a charter and be approved by the PMO before they could be staffed. In addition, the PMO was charged with:

- Tracking all projects on a monthly basis

- Facilitating post-project reviews and distributing the lessons learned

- Assisting in matching project managers to projects

The chemical company now follows the dictum, "Fight fewer battles but win more of them." Its success rate is now 75 percent and the ROI from improvement has doubled. That's successful federalism in action.

SMARTER ENTERPRISE SOLUTION SUMMARY

- Synergy is the only way traditional organizations can win. Feudalism is the problem; integration is the solution.

- Strengthen the core with stronger governing processes.

- Revitalize the strategic planning process so that it illuminates the entire organization.

- Develop clear strategic principles that address the Three Great Tensions: Whom do we serve? What is the role of the center vs. the parts? How should you allocate resources between today and tomorrow?

CHAPTER 10
SMART YOU

"We are all lying in the gutter, but some of us are looking at the stars."

Oscar Wilde

Let's talk about **you**, perhaps a smart person in a dumb organization. Most of this book has been focused on organizations, but at the end of the day, it's people like you that actually do the work. While much this book is targeted at your analytic left brain, your emotional right hemisphere is equally important, especially in terms of your emotional connection to your employer.

How do you feel about your organization? Is it frustrating when you can't use your brain on the job or when you can't get support for your improvement ideas? Do you get angry when you're excluded from decision making? When politics and personal power interfere with doing a good job, does it make you want to check out and operate on autopilot?

You must feel terrible when you can't bring your best to your job. So what can you do? Aside from leaving to find a smarter employer, your best option is to start making your organization smarter and more successful.

You need to enlist in the army of change. Start a revolution. Join those in your organization who stand for the future and not the past. Push a smart agenda and find smart ways to use data whenever and wherever you can. Be the squeaky wheel agitating for improvement. Knock down a few castle walls and help integrate your organization's fiefdoms. Your real job is to improve your organization. It will make your organization a better place.

You'll be fighting the good fight. While you're at it, here are a few final tactics for smart survival.

- Whatever you're doing, first get the data, then think, then act. Resist the temptation of fire-ready-aim. Make a habit of grounding your actions in considered thought. There's no action or decision that can't be made better with information.

- Take time every single day for deep thinking, no matter what trade-offs are needed. Block off *"thinking"* time on your calendar and protect it. Encourage everyone around you to do the same. If you had 30 minutes extra every day, how would you use it? More email? Another meeting? Or reflecting on your job, your organization, and your customers? Time is a gift; use it well.

- Never let the urgent drive out the important. Stop managing symptoms; instead, solve the deep and hidden causes of problems. Let real priorities shape your time.

- Test early and often. The real world is far more complex than can be imagined in a conference room. Beware of group think; shared data doesn't provide certainty, only validation does. Don't repeat your inevitable mistakes; make them early, and learn from them.

- Don't strive for perfection. Voltaire was right: *"The perfect is the enemy of the good."* Pareto was a wimp—it's not 80/20, it's 90/10 that should govern your scope. Stay flexible, because you will never ever have enough data.

- As Winston Churchill proclaimed, *"Never give up, never*

give up." Everything can and must be made better. The status quo is never good enough.

- Take the Serenity Prayer seriously. This wonderful wisdom authored by the American theologian Reinhold Niebuhr states:

Grant me the serenity to accept the things I cannot change,
The courage to change the things I can,
And the wisdom to know the difference.

Your new organization needs your brains to participate in its new nervous system and your capabilities for "betterment" to constantly push for change. It needs you to help it get smarter.

Acknowledgments

First, I want to express my deep appreciation for the perfect proofreading of my wife Pat Stanton and the extraordinary editing of Fiona Luis. Thanks to them I have, hopefully a readable book. I also want to thank Asha Hossein for her wonderful cover design and Sue Balcer for terrific typesetting.

Next, I'd like to thank my business partners Walter Popper and Brad Power for their support and insights.

I'm deeply indebted for the gracious feedback from reviewers Glenn Mangurian, Tim Collins, Jeff DeWolf, SeanMun Liang, Constantine Kazakos, Doug Drollet, and Jim Sinur.

I also wish to express my appreciation for the wisdom of my interviewees and sources including: Lon Blumenthal, John Donlon, Onika Williams, Althea Gill, Tom Waite, Frank Capek, Vanessa DiMaura, Jim Champy, Jim Ware, Dan Markovitz, Michael Procopia, Steve Markman, Rob Sher, Bob Buday, Chunka Mui, Ron Donovan, Peter Schoof, Doron Hai, Steve Shapiro, John Donlon.

Finally, I want to thank all of my students across all those years and organizations. Without your smart questions and stories, I wouldn't have much to say.

www.ingramcontent.com/pod-product-compliance
Lightning Source LLC
Chambersburg PA
CBHW060026210326
41520CB00009B/1022